SECOND EDITION

THE BEGINNING

TEACHER

AT WORK

by

Charles D. Neal
Southern Illinois University
Carbondale, Illinois

Gordon K. Butts
Southern Illinois University
Carbondale, Illinois

J.D. Clemmons
Illinois State University
Normal, Illinois

Burgess Publishing Company
426 South Sixth Street • Minneapolis, Minnesota 55415

DEDICATED

To the millions of men and women in the teaching profession throughout the world whose skills and untiring efforts are bringing knowledge with understanding to the billions of boys and girls of school age.

Copyright © 1971, 1959 by Charles D. Neal
Printed in the United States of America
Library of Congress Catalog Card Number 73-166943
SBN 8087-1417-1

1 2 3 4 5 6 7 8 9 0

Preface

Whether you are a Laboratory Experience Student, Student Teacher, or a First-Year Teacher

The Beginning Teacher at Work puts the elementary and secondary teaching scene in the palm of your hand.

EVERY HOUR THE roster lengthens, name by name. Smith . . . McNeal . . . Rosenberg . . . Snowden . . . Chrapkiewicz . . . Koehler . . . Saphonelli . . . each enter the teaching profession hopeful to meet the challenges of youth living in an everchanging world. This handbook provides many of the practical answers to problems faced by the beginning teacher. It may be used in many ways: First, it should serve as a guide to the college student in his pre-laboratory experiences (1) when he is attempting to evaluate good teaching during observation of other teachers and (2) when he is obtaining actual experience in partial teaching situations. Second, it should provide the student teacher with a resume of practical answers to his teaching problems. Third, it should provide the first year teacher on the job with practical suggestions, which should lead to better teaching practices.

This handbook should also prove beneficial to both supervising and cooperating teachers who supervise student teachers. It should also prove helpful to building principals and special area supervisors of elementary and secondary schools who desire to provide useful information in concise form to their first-year teachers.

ACKNOWLEDGMENTS

We are deeply indebted to the many college professors, supervisors of student teachers, college students, and elementary and secondary school administrators who were kind enough to complete the questionnaire relative to the original manuscript sent nationwide. We have drawn extensively upon their suggestions and recommendations as well as personal conversations with many of them. We regret that it is not possible because of space limitations to give proper individual credit for a job well done.

We are especially grateful for the guidance and counseling given in the organization of the text materials by so many of our good friends, members of the Association of Student Teaching.

We are greatly indebted to Mrs. Sally Sowell, Director of the Gifted Program, Granite City, Illinois Public Schools, for her highly significant contributions to Chapter 3, "Creativity in the Classroom."

Photographs were furnished by authors, Charles D. Neal and Gordon K. Butts, and by Photographic Service, Southern Illinois University, Carbondale.

Finally, it is a particularly gratifying pleasure to acknowledge the indispensable contribution of the following team of teacher education specialists at Illinois State University, Normal: Mr. Dwight O. Coblentz, Mrs. Virginia Hager, Mr. Stephen D. Heider, Mr. William Houston, Dr. Quinn L. Hrudka, Mr. John F. McAteer, Dr. Gene S. McCreery, and Mrs. Ella L. McCumber. Their enlightened review policies and their professional attitude during the final preparation of the manuscript have played a key role in helping to make this book a practical and meaningful message to the millions of young men and women about to engage or beginning to engage in the world's largest vocation — the teaching profession.

October 1, 1971   C.D.N.
                                                                                  G.K.B.
                                                                                  J.D.C.

Contents

Chapter 6 — Instructional Materials

Chapter 7 — Desirable Experiences

Chapter 1

Orientation to Beginning Teaching

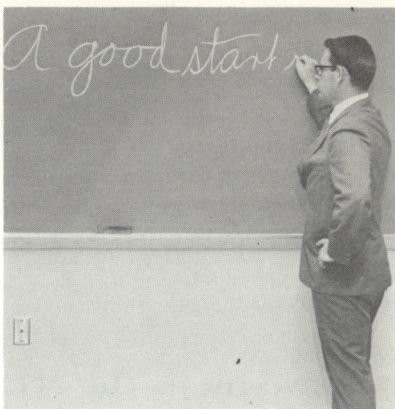

INTRODUCTION

THIS BOOK IS designed for the college student doing laboratory experiences,[1] the student teacher, and the first-year teacher on the job. It does not treat any one specific phase of teacher education exhaustively but rather attempts to supply useful material in various teaching areas with the object of enabling the beginning teacher to help each of his students to progress on a level most suited to his ability. It avoids unnecessary technicalities and confines information to what is essential for elementary and secondary school teachers. In short, it seeks to illustrate a philosophy of teaching and a knowledge of the objectives of education as they relate to the beginning teacher.

At this time many questions are probably running through your mind. "Am I ready?" "For the first time in my college career I shall be 'on the other side of the desk.' What will I really do?" "Will the boys and girls accept me as a teacher?" "How much help can I expect from the person charged with supervising me?" These are natural questions to ask oneself on the threshold of a new experience. You *are* ready to begin teaching! You have had a good background of various subject matter areas and professional courses. The fact that you have been accepted for your assignment means that other personnel think you are ready. They have indicated their belief in you by giving their stamp of approval. As for being nervous and having many questions running through your mind, you should know that you have plenty of company. Most beginning teachers approach their teaching assignment with somewhat mixed emotions. At this very moment there are literally thousands of educators in much the same position as yourself, contemplating the outcome of their

---

[1] "Laboratory experiences" are certain education courses (prior to student teaching) in which the college student combines theory learned in the classroom with some actual teaching on the elementary or secondary level.

teaching assignment. For instance, the beginning teacher in the picture is making sure that he is ready. Among his other preparations for his first day, he came to school early. Writing "A good start makes for a good ending" on the chalkboard gave him a certain amount of personal satisfaction but, more important, this slogan served later as a kickoff remark to his class, teaching them the importance of getting a good start on their class work.

Although you may feel that you are ready, you will profit more from your beginning teaching experiences if you have a clear understanding of your role. This chapter is designed to help you get off to a good start. You will want to read carefully the suggestions made in the pages which follow and to discuss them with your supervisory personnel, who will work closely with you.

OBJECTIVES FOR THE BEGINNING TEACHER

Teaching is much more than an opportunity to instruct by the trial-and-error method. It should enrich your future career with a series of fruitful experiences, and it was with this goal in mind that the following list of objectives for the beginning teacher was drawn up:

1. To provide opportunities for assessing your philosophy in terms of that which you encounter.

2. To provide opportunities for your improvement in teaching-learning situations.

3. To provide opportunities for using methods, techniques, and instructional materials so that you can become a successful teacher.

4. To provide opportunities for improvement of your professional interests, attitudes, ideas, and techniques of teaching through self-evaluation.

5. To provide opportunities for continuous evaluation by your students and supervising personnel of your effectiveness as a teacher.

6. To provide opportunities for you to understand the actual working conditions of the school, which will include acquaintance with school board policies, regulations, committees, records, reports, and other mechanical aspects of the school.

7. To provide opportunities for you to observe and participate in extraclass or cocurricular activities.

8. To provide opportunities for you to become aware of the importance of human relations as they apply to the students, faculty, parents, nonteaching personnel, and members of the community at large.

9. To provide opportunities for you to recognize and make allowances for individual differences among your students.

10. To provide opportunities for you to gain experience in working effectively with students from different ethnic groups as you become familiar with their problems.

PHILOSOPHY OF TEACHING

Your professional experience thus far has probably shown you that teaching practices vary widely among many distinguished college professors as well as outstanding public school teachers and administrators. If you have made this discovery, you are well on your way toward becoming a successful teacher. If not, you should plan to learn more about the philosophy of education. You will find that there are a variety of school practices — all well defended by both teachers and administrators. Although many schools use standard nomenclature for subjects taught, few teach the same subject matter or employ the same techniques or methods in the same way. For example, some teachers seem to ignore drill while others seem to stress it. Some seem to have many extraclass activities, others only a few. Some stress the pragmatic, others the traditional approach. We could go on and on — the differences seem to exist. Sometimes you will ask yourself if everyone is wrong but you. There is a practical explanation for the wide differences found among school systems, namely that there is no one, single, basic philosophy of education. Nevertheless, the differences found among public schools are not sufficient to imply many vastly different philosophies in operation in the American educational system.

The philosophy of teaching can be defined as a body of principles underlying a specific branch of learning. For example, when you attempt to make your teaching intelligible, you are exposing your particular philosophy by explaining *why, what,* and *how* things should be taught. It is therefore important that you understand the philosophy of the school in which you teach if you are to meet your students' needs through their mental, physical, social, emotional, and moral development. The following is an example of what may happen when a beginning teacher fails to understand the philosophy of the school in which he teaches:

Jerry B., a high school student teacher, believed that a permissive atmosphere should prevail in the classroom at all times. Actually he formulated his philosophy from several visitation days when he observed a teacher operating in a school system where permissiveness by both pupils and teachers was the rule rather than the exception. Moreover, Jerry seemed to idolize this particular teacher and everything that he did. Thus he based his entire philosophy of teaching on one situation. Unfortunately, Jerry began teaching in a school system which favored the traditional school philosophy. Jerry's belief in the effectiveness of a permissive atmosphere in the classroom was so deep-seated that figuratively he threw limited expression "out of the window." Actually the pupils had a series of field days until the situation became so out of control that one of the supervising personnel had to take complete charge. When Jerry was able to understand that change for improvement requires time and that the philosophy of a particular school cannot be disrupted by immediate changes without all concerned having a complete understanding, he was permitted to assume full responsibility again.

BEGINNING TEACHER RESPONSIBILITIES

As a beginning teacher, you will have certain responsibilities that are associated with certain freedoms afforded a teacher. Your success and the amount of freedom you are given will depend on how you handle your various responsibilities. As you demonstrate your ability to shoulder more and more responsibility successfully you will find that more and more freedom to do the kind of teaching you desire will come your way. Coupled closely with accepting responsibility is the *ability* to perform successfully the various jobs that make up the teaching assignment. Here are six guidelines to help you to understand better certain important abilities required of a beginning teacher.

Teaching success depends upon your ability —

1. to improve your skill in the techniques of lesson planning.
2. to improve your skill in the techniques of teaching.
3. to improve your skill in evaluation of your students and in self-evaluation.
4. to improve your skill in maintaining good relationships with your colleagues, parents, and members of your community as well as your students.
5. to improve your background of knowledge both in your teaching field and in general areas of popular interest.
6. to improve your ability to be patient, understanding, and persistent when situations do not move along as you think they should.

After thinking about his responsibilities, one beginning teacher developed "The Daily Dozen," which follows, as a check on his ability to succeed. How many of the twelve items can you check "yes"? How many more will you be able to check "yes" as the school term progresses? Unless you can honestly check all twelve with a "yes" by the end of the semester, you should seek help from your supervisor.

THE DAILY DOZEN —

1. Do I place school duties and responsibilities ahead of personal wishes and desires and accept cheerfully all reasonable duties assigned me?   yes   no

2. Do I strive to exemplify the attitudes and actions of a teacher rather than those of a student?   yes   no

3. Do I conform to school regulations and policies and to local standards of behavior?   yes · no

4. Do I report for all school appointments and duties on time?   yes   no

5. Do I plan all work and submit such plans to my supervising personnel when requested?   yes   no

6. Do I safeguard all personal and confidential information concerning my students and use it only for professional purposes?   yes   no

7. Do I follow the rules of basic courtesy toward school administrators, teachers, pupils, nonacademic personnel, and members of the community?   yes   no

8. Do I have an appreciative attitude toward all services rendered in my behalf?   yes   no

9. Do I dress appropriately according to faculty standards?   yes   no

10. Do I endeavor continuously to discover and correct my shortcomings?   yes   no

11. Do I avoid all partiality and favoritism toward my students?   yes   no

12. Do I strive for personal and professional growth through continued study and effort?   yes   no

The foregoing digest of responsibilities is intended only to provide a short orientation at the outset of the school term. More specific responsibilities will be explained in detail in the chapters which follow.

PROFESSIONAL ORGANIZATIONS

Have you ever wondered why the medical and legal professions, to mention only two, are held in high esteem by Mr. John Q. Public? The reason is quite simple. Many years ago medical doctors and lawyers learned that if a profession is to earn public respect it is essential that its members have the highest respect for each other and also for their profession. The American Medical Association is one example of an organization that has developed high standards of conduct. Medical men today are subject to constant evaluation and must meet extremely high standards from both the moral and medical point of view. Members who are guilty of "shady practices," use out-of-date techniques, show disrespect for fellow practitioners, or otherwise behave disreputably are driven out of the profession — not necessarily by law, but by the members of the Association itself with the consent of its officers.

During the past quarter of a century the teaching profession has improved its standards significantly. Many of the state laws responsible for improved conditions were passed thanks to the combined efforts of powerful local, state, and national teacher associations. Nevertheless, teaching still has a long way to go if it is to attain the heights reached by the professions mentioned above. In fact, this will be possible only when all teachers are required to be members of an accredited association demanding high standards from both moral and educational points of view. You and other beginning teachers can do much to help your profession reach that stage, or you can sit idly by and permit it to lag or even regress. Actually, more than you may think depends on you as a professional person — your entire future is at stake. What do you intend to do about it?

There are a number of local, state, and national teachers' organizations for you to follow. Two of the foremost national organizations are the National Education Association and the American Federation of Teachers. Do you know which of these organizations you wish to support? Are you ready to make a decision in the event you do not belong to either?

Sometimes teachers find it easier to go along with the crowd than to think for themselves before acting. As a beginning teacher, you should want to join and support the professional organization of your choice. Begin by gathering the facts on both the N.E.A. and the A.F.T. Among other facts study the code of ethics of each organization.

Once you have the facts, discuss the problem with your colleagues. When you feel you have the answer, join and support the organization which you feel has the power to help the teaching profession reach its rightful place in our great American society.

AVAILABLE OUT-OF-SCHOOL FACILITIES

At a recent "rap" session of beginning teachers only, Jane S. was asked to describe her most outstanding experience. This is her story:

During the evening of my second day as a beginning teacher, I was invited to a Saturday night party with other young people in the community. Among other things during the evening, "pot" was passed around. I lit a "joint" along with the rest of the group, for long ago I decided that I couldn't care less what the local "yokels" thought about my private life. The first thing Monday morning I found out what the "yokels" do in cases like mine. Several older members of the community telephoned the principal, and he was waiting for me when I arrived at school. He was quick to inform me that the community frowns on "pot" parties and that he agreed with them.

Perhaps this is an extreme case of a beginning teacher going off the deep end. However, each community has its own customs and traditions. Find out what the social facilities are in the community in which you are about to teach. It would be best to find out about them before accepting a teaching assignment. Then if the community did not have the kinds of facilities you desire, you could seek another teaching assignment in a community more compatible with your way of life.

OFF TO A GOOD START?

Below is a check-list which you will want to check prior to your first day of teaching. If you can truthfully answer 17 or more of the statements with the answer "yes," you will be off to a good start in your career as a teacher.

BEGINNING TEACHER READINESS CHECK-LIST –

1. Have an understanding of the purpose, objectives, and philosophy of teaching. yes no

2. Have acquired a basic knowledge of child growth and development, along with desirable professional "tool" courses. yes no

3. Have mastered the subject matter required in both major and minor teaching fields. yes no

4. Have acquired skill in making subject matter meaningful to children. yes no

5. Have developed acceptable personal behavior patterns. yes no

6. Have learned to act and to dress in good taste. yes no

7. Have developed a pleasing personality particularly suited to the classroom. yes no

8. Have acquired a knowledge of direction of at least one extra-class activity. yes no

9. Have acquired skill in putting into practice oral and written expression. yes no

10. Have acquired skill in administering, grading, and interpreting "teacher-made" and standardized tests. yes no

11. Have acquired an understanding of group processes as they apply to teaching. yes no

12. Have acquired an understanding of the factors involved in the utilization of instructional materials as they apply to student learning. yes no

13. Have made plans to become familiar with the instructional materials of the school. yes no

14. Have made plans to meet parents in homes, PTA meetings, and school conferences. yes no

15. Have made plans to study, with a purpose, a cumulative record of each student.   yes   no

16. Have made plans to study the community as it pertains to the improvement of student learning.   yes   no

17. Have made plans to become familiar with other academic and nonacademic personnel.   yes   no

18. Have made plans to learn the complete layout of the physical plant — offices, storage space, duplicating facilities, cafeteria, washrooms, nurse's room, etc.   yes   no

19. Have made plans to learn both student and teacher rules, regulations, and policies.   yes   no

20. Have made plans to develop a day-by-day log or a running account of all teaching experiences.   yes   no

REFERENCES

Radebaugh, B. J. "Student teachers, knowledge and effective teaching behavior," *Journal of Teacher Education,* Summer 1970, 21:173-7.

Bills, A. "Professionalism begins with student teaching," *Clearing House,* November 1970, 45:156-60.

Adams, R. D. "Problems of student teachers," *School and Community,* May 1969, 55:10.

Reeves, E. "Those faltering first steps of practice," *Education Supervision,* August 30, 1968, 2780:359.

Chapter 2

Classroom Management

INTRODUCTION

HOW WILL YOUR students react to your classroom? Will they find it pleasant, attractive, and well-organized? Will they find it a place where they understand the rules of the room as well as those for the entire school plant? How will they find you, their teacher, as a person? Do you care about students? How they react? What they like as well as what they dislike? What attitudes, habits, and abilities have they achieved — some positive, some negative? If you can truthfully answer positively to such questions as these, your students will not join the thousands of public-school graduates and dropouts who look back with horror on their frustrating experiences in the classroom.

There are many and varied factors in operation which have a direct bearing upon the learning situation. Some of these can be anticipated through careful planning; others must be resolved as they occur. As you direct the class, provisions must be made in your planning to regulate as many of these influences as possible. Many can actually be controlled by you — the teacher.

Successful teachers have discovered that well thought out answers to certain specific questions are most helpful in assuring sound practices in guiding the learning environment. Following are eight such basic questions considered important by one successful teacher. The authors suggest you make a list of these, jotting down bits of information on each one as answers occur to you during your teaching assignment.

1. What is your plan for the formation of correct habits for yourself and for your students to ensure successful classroom operation?

2. What does a pleasant physical classroom environment have to do with learning, and what can you do about providing for it?

3. What is discipline, and when is your classroom well-disciplined, according to the philosophy of the school in which you teach?

4. Just what are the legal rights of teachers as provided by the School Code of the state in which you teach?

5. How does the implementation of democratic techniques on the classroom level influence learning?

6. Does the wise use and proper care of supplies and reference materials have any effect on learning and, if so, to what extent?

7. Just how does general housekeeping of the classroom enhance or retard the learning situation?

8. What can you do to provide for student health and safety?

To provide a basis for direction of your classroom each of the following topics in this chapter is devoted to providing assistance in answering one of the above questions.

CORRECT HABITS

Just what can you do toward the formation of correct habits for yourself and for your pupils to ensure successful classroom operation? Let's see if we can come up with some answers to this question. To begin with, in everyday speech the word "habit" refers mainly to an extensively practiced and well-established manner of behavior, but in educational psychology it refers to all the products of learning. Therefore, you and your students will function in a certain way, each differing from each other, depending upon past learning or experience. It follows, then, that as learning continues, habits will change. This concept requires that a learner must keep an open mind, and it also insists that he modify his "habits" or behavior as a result of new information.

Your primary concern in the development of correct habits is that learning begins with the student's problems, not the teacher's. Your success in directing the learning activities of the class depends upon your recognizing and understanding the real problems faced by the students in your group. Also, it stands to reason that the formation of your own habits, as they pertain to classroom management, should be as a means to an end — that of teaching good learning habits to your students.

The development of your habits of planning, organizing, and presenting materials should be such that they indicate your basic assumption — namely, that learning is not a matter of performing for teachers, but rather is a process in which the learners must be actively engaged. Learning is an experiencing by the learner and without experience there is no learning. You as the classroom leader can develop correct professional habits for this function of your work if you have an open mind, for an open mind is receptive to new ideas for making improvements, resulting in the formation of better habits.

The second point to consider in improving your manner of teaching is that learning is an individual concern. Therefore you need to understand and put into practice the basic principles of learning to which you were exposed in your college methods and psychology courses.

PHYSICAL CLASSROOM ENVIRONMENT

What does a pleasant physical classroom environment have to do with learning, and what can you do about providing it? Research findings show that factors such as lighting, heating, ventilation, and general room arrangement play a significant role in the learning climate. Educators have discovered that under good physical conditions students not only learn better but also conduct themselves in a manner which makes better learning possible.

The remainder of this section is for the elementary teacher, since it is elementary-school oriented.

It does not require the presence of a professionally educated person to know when the classroom is too cold or too hot, when it is too dark, when there is a glare, or when a generally appealing appearance is lacking. One of your problems in preparing to become a good elementary teacher is to notice undesirable classroom features immediately and to remedy them as rapidly as possible.

A successful teacher automatically considers the arrangement of the furniture and rearranges it if necessary. For example, most successful teachers have at least one "beauty spot" in the room. Is this true of *your* classroom? You may also want to provide for a number of interest centers about the room. A science center is one such example. Here a physical setup indicates the types of experiences in science the students have been encountering, such as a display table containing deciduous tree leaves, evergreen needles, acorns, twigs, etc., which they have brought in in connection with a study unit on trees.

If you are teaching in a modern school that provides its classrooms with movable desks, tables, and chairs, reference materials, potted flowers, goldfish, etc., it should be a pleasant task to arrange these pieces to ensure greater aesthetic attraction as well as the best educational advantages for the students.

DISCIPLINE

What is discipline, and when is your classroom well disciplined? Dr. Carter Good offers six definitions of discipline. The one we have selected as most applicable to the word as we use it here is "The process or result of directing or subordinating immediate wishes, impulses, desires, or interests for the sake of an ideal or for the purpose of gaining more effective, dependable action."[1]

---

[1] Carter Good, Editor, *Dictionary of Education.* New York: McGraw-Hill Book Company, 1945.

In simple language, *discipline* is a matter of establishing control or rapport with your students. Of course, the same discipline techniques do not work the same way for each teacher. The personality of the individual teacher determines to a great extent how he will discipline his class.

Discipline is probably the topic which is most pressing, most popular, and most misunderstood by parents, teachers, and school administrators. But if you can think of discipline problems as being to the teacher much like a high or low temperature is to the physician you are on the correct path to understanding them. They are always symptomatic of something wrong with the positive side of teaching. And do not be surprised if finding solutions to some "problem children" seems next to impossible.

Good discipline and good learning conditions are actually one and the same thing. The best way to face unsatisfactory discipline is to devote oneself wholeheartedly to the problem of providing the best positive learning situations possible.

Students kept busily engaged in meaningful and worthwhile activities seldom become discipline problems.

Beginning the teaching assignment with a conviction that you must have discipline at all costs is a defensive reaction and should be discarded. All who follow the game of football have learned that, as also in many other contests, the best *defense* is a good *offense.* The same reasoning applies in teaching. If you can create an active, interesting learning atmosphere, a powerful educational offense will have been developed. More on *how* to establish the learning climate is brought out in the chapters to follow.

The strongest force for individual control is the opinion of the group of which the individual is a member. It is so in your classroom. If a standard of conduct is arrived at with the help and approval of the class, any individual will be reluctant to depart from it. Your problem, then, is to build correct group attitudes. For example, if proper group attitudes have been built relative to impulsive verbal blasts, the pupil who continues to let off such blasts will probably feel the coolness of the class members toward him. This peer reaction will encourage behavior improvement.

If you have students who do not respond to the above methods of control (as in any society there are some), you must of necessity adopt other means of bringing these pupils back into an approved form of behavior. This action should always be regarded as a corrective measure, not as a punishment. Revenge is a poor motive and has no place in the teaching profession.

It follows then that the nature of the individual as well as the character of the offense should determine the action you must follow. It should also be pointed out that you operate with authority, standing in "loco parentis" while the child is in school. The term *loco parentis* is defined in *Black's Law Dictionary* as follows: "In place of a parent; instead of a parent; charged, factitiously, with a parent's rights, duties, and responsibilities."[2]

As a teacher you have the responsibility during school hours of disciplining your students. Also, many of the courts have agreed that this right to discipline students includes the use of corporal punishment. If your board of education approves, you have a right to inflict reasonable punishment for misconduct, including corporal punishment. However, you are never permitted to inflict punishment maliciously, particularly without provocation. Nothing can be interpreted as reasonable punishment when the motive is malicious. Punishment can only be administered for a salutary purpose to maintain the discipline and efficiency expected of a particular school.

Finally, take note of this: Most school districts actually fear law suits if a child is mistreated or mishandled. Before taking any physical action be sure to have at least one adult, besides yourself, as a witness. Also, remember that neither you nor anyone else can predict a jury's verdict if a parent decides to question a disciplinary action by taking the matter to court.

---

[2] *Black's Law Dictionary,* 4th ed. St. Paul, Minnesota: West Publishing Co., 1951, p. 896.

TEACHERS' LEGAL AUTHORITY

Do state laws provide for legal rights of teachers? They most certainly do. And one of the first "dos" on your list should be to secure a copy of your state school code and become familiar with your legal rights as a teacher. Usually, copies may be had for the asking from the county or state superintendent's office.

Honest, sincere teachers are usually assisted in legal matters pertaining to teaching. For instance, many of the states provide group insurance of various kinds through their state education associations, and a number of states permit school boards to buy insurance of one sort or another for their teachers. Policies sometimes cover hospitalization, surgical and medical expenses, accidental death, term life, straight life, and even professional liability.

The matter of school discipline as described in the previous topic is one of the superintendent's functions after board policy has been established. Legally, neither you, the principal, nor the superintendent can make rules relative to expulsion of students. This function belongs to the board of education. If the behavior of certain students warrants expulsion, you should inform the proper administrator. It is his duty to enforce the board's policy regarding pupil conduct, but he usually does so on the recommendations of the teacher or teachers concerned.

As to your own legal rights, your greatest concern is probably with personal liability. Check your own state school law on "teacher liability" and be sure that you understand when a teacher is subject to liability in your state. While you may not have heard of a case where a teacher has appeared in court as the defendant, it is nevertheless a fact that teachers occasionally find themselves the target of complaints and have to appear in court.

DEMOCRATIC TECHNIQUES

Does the implementation of democratic techniques on the classroom level influence learning? (For a more complete treatment of teaching techniques see Chapter V, "Teaching Techniques.") First let us review the three major types, or *means,* of classroom management attitudes of teachers. One is known as the democratic group means; here the teacher and pupils share problems and information and work together toward common goals. The second is known as the autocratic means; here goals are handed down with participation of those who are to be affected. The third is the "laissez faire" means, which follows a disorganized or "let-alone" pattern.

Certainly there are places in our culture, as for example in the armed forces, where the autocratic means seems most appropriate. In our present day, school teachers are more and more implementing the democratic type of organization in their classroom work. You will want to work with these kinds of teachers.

The proponents of this practice do not simply make an assignment and recite in which the lines of communication run in one direction, namely, only from teacher to student. Rather they use what is sometimes called the interactive group process, in which the children may all take a part and interact more freely, as in a planning period. Since, as mentioned earlier in this chapter, children learn what they experience, this becomes an important kind of learning. In a democratic activity they learn how to work together toward —

1. Attaining common goals.
2. Achieving solutions.
3. Delegating action.
4. Obtaining productivity through the democratic or group processes.

In many of the education experiments that have been conducted in recent years, such techniques seem to lead to higher levels of productivity. Therefore, you will be wise to organize and plan your particular work along democratic lines.

CLASSROOM HOUSEKEEPING

Just how does general housekeeping of the classroom enhance or retard the learning situation? Classroom management involves a number of things, among them being caring for the physical aspects of the school room. Every classroom reflects the teacher's personality. Since a good teacher works with students five or six hours a day, he will be eager to make the room neat (that is, except for the times when constructive activities are being done), clean, cheerful, and attractive. You will wish to make your students feel happy and content by maintaining pleasant surroundings for them. They, too, will wish to have a part in the responsibilities that make such a pleasant classroom. A superintendent recently emphasized the importance of classroom housekeeping when he said, "I can give a good evaluation of the kind of teacher occupying a classroom just by visiting it after the teacher has gone home, providing both teacher and janitor leave it intact at the end of the day."

The things that make an attractive classroom are not difficult to obtain. Many beautiful and interesting pictures may be collected from current periodicals, newspapers, advertising circulars, and calendars. These may be arranged on bulletin boards. Similarly, it is always a joy to watch plants take root and grow from slips that students have brought in, and these plants give the room a homelike touch. At the elementary level there may be interesting corners or shelves where science and nature study specimens can be arranged. A small comfortable reading nook or corner is a pleasant place in which students can browse during their leisure time.

When work is done, you will naturally want to keep your classroom neat and clean. Chalkboards should be clean and orderly; chalk and erasers should be provided, waste baskets should be cared for, and other housekeeping duties should be punctually attended to. Student committees may help with such things as keeping the reading corner in order, dusting the room, placing the furniture, caring for the plants, arranging the bulletin boards, etc.

PUBLIC HEALTH AND SAFETY

What can the teacher do to provide for student health and safety? One beginning teacher's reaction to this question was, "We have a school nurse; why should I worry about the health and safety of my kids?" School nurse or not, this teacher was greatly misinformed, to say the least.

Your cooperation with the school nurse is a double check on the health and safety of your youngsters. But there is much more for the teacher "who cares."

Again referring to the school code of your state, you will find out exactly what is legally expected of you as a teacher. For instance, most states require instruction on tobacco and alcohol. Usually, certain areas pertaining to the government and history of America are specified. When the school plant was constructed certain legal matters as to amount of space per student, lighting, heating, ventilation, fire protection, and the like had to be met by the architect who designed the building. So on and on go the state school codes with respect to the health and safety of your students.

There are things other than specified health and safety laws for the teacher to think about during the teaching day. For instance, the penalty for teachers' negligence is sometimes reflected adversely in the students' health and safety. As a case in point, one sixth grade teacher knowingly allowed the boys to play ball with a broken bat. "This bat is OK," said the teacher. "It only has the knob broken off." True, that was all that was wrong with it, but it was enough to cause one of the batters to accidently lose control of the bat. Sailing through the air, it struck another youngster in the back of the head, causing a brain concussion. Fortunately for the teacher, a trial jury ruled the injury an accident, saving the teacher X number of dollars in liability payments. Was it an accident? The authors say, "No. The teacher should have used better judgment."

Here are some other judgments a teacher should involve himself with during the course of the teaching day. He should check the room temperature and make sure that the ventilation is right. For example, one teacher might be "cold natured." He can simply put on more clothes, rather than raise the thermostat above a temperature comfortable for the children. To study satisfactorily, a student should be in a well-ventilated and properly heated room. Listlessness is often traceable to the teacher's disregard for these fundamental concerns of good classroom management. You will also wish to make sure that each student's desk and chair is adjusted for his comfort and ease in working. Those students who have slight hearing and vision defects should be given special consideration in the seating plan. And, of course, the light should be of adequate foot candles. The teacher should guard against glares and harmful reflection of light. He should also be prompt in turning on artificial lights when they are necessary.

One beginning teacher made a study, gathering the specifics with respect to the "other judgments" as mentioned above. So that the information would be readily available, she listed it on "3 x 5" cards. The following are some of the points she covered on these cards:

1. Temperature: classroom — 68-72 degrees Fahrenheit; shops and laboratories, slightly lower; locker rooms and swimming pools — approximately 80 degrees.

2. Circulation. Air should be in constant circulation. Be certain fresh air is coming into the room and foul air is leaving. Check for noxious odors, fumes, and dust — step out into the hall for three minutes. On entering the room the nose will tell the story.

3. Humidity. Generally, humidity should range between 40 and 60 per cent. (The teacher bought a cheap humidity and temperature gauge, which she kept on her desk.)

4. Lighting. Some lighting experts claim 100 foot candles per student is necessary. One practical educator says, "Seeing depends upon the kind of work to be done, eyesight of the students, brightness of the light, reflection and glare, color of the equipment, furniture, and the room itself."

5. Cleanliness. This is a two-way street. Both the teacher and students should make every effort to keep the floor free of paper and excessive dirt. True, the custodian has the job of cleaning the building, and his job is a big one. No use making it bigger than ever by allowing the students to develop negative health and safety habits rather than positive ones. And the custodian will think more of you for the added cooperation!

At the close of the period, the students should leave the classroom in an orderly manner. To ensure this, you must establish a reasonable procedure in advance, and make sure the students understand what is expected from them. Young children have to be reminded of such safety rules as keeping to the right, especially going up and down stairs, and of the danger involved in running up and down stairs and through the corridors. The teacher must also assume the responsibility for guiding the students in developing good and safe habits of movement in groups. To do this properly, you should become familiar with the traffic rules and regulations, not only of the classroom, but also of the entire building.

REFERENCES

Wesley, D. A. "Classroom control should be a vital part of teacher education," *Clearing House,* Fall 1971, 45:346-9.

Lowry, W. H., and R. R. Reilley, "Life problems and interests of adolescents," *Clearing House,* November 1970, 45:164-8.

Geddes, C. L., and B. Y. Kool, "Instructional management system for classroom teachers," *Elementary School Journal,* April 1969, 69:337-45.

Cantrell, M. L. "Power of positive teaching," *Instructor,* fall 1969, 78:72.

Chapter 3

Creativity in the Classroom

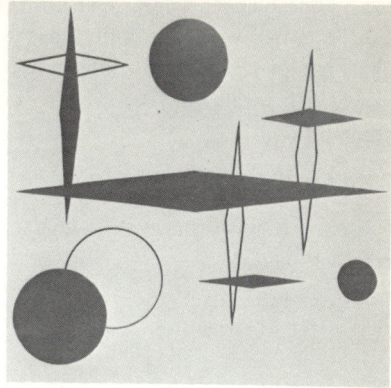

INTRODUCTION

"THERE IS SO much being said and written about creativity today, not only in the fine arts, but in education, business, industry, and in living itself," said Mr. Brown recently to his son's teacher. Then Mr. Brown went on to raise two questions: "What is creativity?" and "What, if anything, is being done to determine the degree of creativity in my son and others in his class?"

As a beginning teacher, what answers would you suggest to Mr. Brown? To be sure, you should have answers to such questions. But, more important, you as a teacher should make a real in-depth study of exactly how you can make the ultimate use of creativity as part of your classroom procedure.

WHAT IS CREATIVITY?

Stated simply, *creativity* consists of a person's ability to bring ideas or things into existence that have not existed as such before. To bring this about in the classroom, you need to remember this challenge to your teaching ability: To become creative, the creator many times borrows from or makes use of ideas or things that have been previously produced. Then he transforms them into something new and different. In short, at least part of creativity is ability to see the world in a new perspective.

Another challenge to your teaching ability is to recognize that the creative mind is a difficult one and, for most teachers, difficult to detect. To be sure, every student in your classroom is endowed with a certain degree of creative ability. Some students possess this ability to a very great degree, others possess it in a moderate degree, while still others possess only a limited ability. Your job is to help each student discover inventiveness, productivity, and revelation of truth to the fullest extent of his creative ability while he is also growing in subject matter knowledge. One rule of thumb to accomplish this is not to become an *uncreative* teacher where "pat answers" are the rule rather than the exception. Furthermore, why not join those teachers who are accepting the classroom challenge of searching for alternate and better methods of teaching? If you do, you will be well on your way to becoming a creative teacher with a creative student body.

WHAT CREATIVITY IS NOT

Now that we have read what creativity *is,* let's take a good look at what creativity is *not:*

1. Creativity is not restricted to place, time, age, or certain segments of the population.

2. Creativity is not a completely new product or idea. It is a reintegration of existing materials with added elements which are new.

3. Creativity is not the same thing as intelligence. Creativity and intelligence are separate endowments that have a very low correlation.

4. Creativity is not the product of unstable persons.

5. Creativity is not primarily a quality of personality. Rather, it is a unique thinking process.

OBJECTIVES

Here are a set of objectives developed by one beginning teacher as they applied to his particular teaching area. Perhaps you can use them as guidelines for developing a set of objectives of your own:

1. The teacher should acquaint himself with the personality traits that characterize creative persons.

2. The teacher should not confuse creativity and academic ability. They are not necessarily synonymous.

3. The teacher should value creativity as much as apparent academic ability.

4. The teacher should not mistake creative behavior for misbehavior.

5. The teacher should seize every opportunity to nurture creative potential.

6. The teacher should not rely solely on one means of identifying creative persons.

7. The teacher should create a climate in which creativity can be freely expressed.

8. The teacher should not feel inferior towards or resent a creative student.

9. The teacher should search for at least one creative personality trait in each individual and use it as a basis for further development.

10. The teacher should not "write off" a student as being uncreative.

Teachers should make every effort to recognize creative abilities, then nurture them to their fullest potential.

CREATIVITY SHOULD EXTEND TO ALL AREAS

Creativity should apply to some extent to all of the classrooms from kindergarten through high school. It is regrettable that to some educators creativity has been associated with only the fields of music, art, and dramatics. For example, if you were to say to some teachers, "This morning I found several students in my class applying creative thinking," your comment would probably bring forth a mental image of some students "beating out" an original tune on the piano, or sweeping a paint brush across a canvas, or writing an original poem or a two-act play. Seldom would your stimulus bring forth a mental picture of some physics students working on a new solution to a scientific problem or some arithmetic students working on a new solution to a problem in a class of elementary mathematics.

You will want to plan your work so that the required facts, skills, and basic understandings will not be neglected. On the other hand, your mind should be open always to giving assistance to creative ideas developed by your students and to the encouragement of creative thinking from the others. For instance, you will want to supplement your teaching by taking advantage of newness and by encouraging students to develop originality as a procedure toward better learning. Above all, you should set examples of creativity through your methods and techniques of teaching. It is seldom good practice to follow set or stereotyped patterns. You will want to pay particular attention to creative teaching when making detailed lesson plans as suggested in Chapter IV, "Instructional Planning." As a further bit of food for thought on the encouragement of student creativity, it should be remembered that your students of today cannot hope to solve all of tomorrow's problems with today's answers.

ORGANIZATIONAL PATTERN FOR THE DEVELOPMENT OF CLASSROOM CREATIVITY

The four factors which will enable you to recognize creativity in your students are fluency, originality, flexibility, and elaboration. In the pages which follow techniques and activities which will encourage your students to demonstrate their possession of these attributes are suggested.

1. Fluency. This falls into three categories:

a. Ideational: The ability to generate a quantity of ideas within a given time or to give ideas that fit a definition. It can best be recognized through problem-solving exercises. For example, divergent thinking can be stimulated by asking questions such as —

What might happen if . . . ?
List or write all the ways . . . .
How many ways . . . ?
How could you . . . ?

b. Associational: The ability to complete relationships, see connections, think in analogies, and understand relationships. The following examples of sentence-writing exercises may give you ideas for developing such exercises for your own teaching area:

Think of all the words that mean the opposite, or nearly opposite, of the word *sad.*
Think of all the words beginning with sta . . .

Think of all the synonyms that would substitute for the underlined words in the following sentence: The <u>frightened</u> boy ran from the <u>tyrannical</u> old man who <u>lived</u> in the <u>mountain</u> valley.

c. Expressional: The ability to construct sentences easily and quickly and to organize ideas into systems. An example of a suitable sentence-writing exercise would be —

Make as many different sentences as possible using all four of the following words: send, almost, show, large.

2. Originality: The ability to produce uncommon responses, unusual or unconventional associations. The following are some examples of classroom activities designed to encourage originality:

a. Language Arts: Tell the students to take three minutes to write a story using the following words in the order in which they appear here: beach, girl, blue, foamy, excited, boat, subdued, sand, alerted, signal.

b. Social Studies:
Discussion or debate on controversial issues.
Ask the class to construct a unit of work on an imaginary country or people.

c. Mathematics:
Magic squares
Construction of mathematical puzzles or games
Paper folding
Ask students to develop their own number system, including definition of operations.

d. Science:
Have the students design their own experiments.
Have the students write science fiction.
Have the students construct models or working objects.

3. Flexibility: The ability to think in various directions. The thinking may be spontaneous (thought striking out in a number of different directions) or adaptive (deliberately changing one's thinking to meet changing situations).

Spontaneous thinking may be stimulated by brainstorming or by having the students list unusual uses of common objects, noting the *shifts* in thinking that occur.

Micro-teaching and focused teaching can be employed to encourage adaptive thinking. Have the students rearrange letters in scrambled words.

4. Elaboration: The ability to specify details that contribute to the development of a general idea. Examples of suitable exercises:
Making up descriptive phrases
Comprehensive role-playing
Changing existing story plots
Developing projects, exhibits, and bulletin boards that tell complete stories

EXAMPLES OF CLASSROOM CREATIVITY

The following examples of creativity in the classroom are given for your consideration. Perhaps they will give you ideas for incorporating creativity in your particular teaching area.

1. Stories in the Lower Grades: Even little children want to be creative and, at an appropriate developmental age, they desire to express themselves in written form. However, the first creative writing may involve little writing on the part of the child. Very young pupils do not have the necessary mechanical skills for writing complete stories, so their creative ventures may be taken as dictation by you as their teacher.

One way to encourage the group toward creative activity might be as you finish reading a story to say, "Some of you may like to make up stories. Perhaps you have already made up some about animals, grownups, or other children. If you have one to tell, we would enjoy hearing it." Another way to encourage creativity might be for you to have individual children dictate to you certain original stories when all the children are working on individual activities that require little teacher supervision. These stories may be shared later, the author willing.

You will find that the characters in stories of the five-year-old, for example, will be much like the people he already knows. He likes animal characters and accepts as fact that most of them talk as human beings.

These two stories were recently told to their class by two small five-year-olds:

> I made a boat.
> I used two pieces of wood.
> One was little.
> One was big.
> I finished it.
>
> My hammer went tap, tap, tap,
> And my saw went SH, sh, SH, sh.
> My boat was finished in a hurry.
> It was a pretty blue boat.

You can readily tell that the first story rather clearly indicates boredom, while the second one expresses the child's emotions along with the obvious pleasure he enjoyed during the activity.

Creative story writing need not necessarily be fancy or unusual, but it must reflect the inner self and express the true feeling of the storyteller's own ideas.

2. Hobbies in the Junior High School: On any level or age, but particularly during preadolescence and adolescence when boys and girls seem to collect, classify, reconstruct, organize, and analyze objects, people, events, and ideas, hobbies can be filled with worthwhile educational experiences for both the individual and the group.

Most teachers believe that hobbies can be justified in any grade or subject through —

a. training for worthwhile use of leisure time.

b. taking care of individual differences.

c. discovering the values of a hobby or hobbies in relation to a particular unit of study.

d. encouraging the development of creativity in the individual.

Hobbies may or may not be creative in themselves, but the activities within often can be a part of the individual's imagination, his own ideas or self-expression — his creativeness.

The following example is of an eighth grade student's creativeness in hobbies which was developed as part of her Social Studies-Language Arts block of time:

The student collected poetry on various subjects, from various authors, and of various styles and forms. Her hobby was her individual collection but, in itself, it was not necessarily creative.

But from this collection the student wrote her own poetry which now actually becomes a part of herself. In developing a particular poem, for example, she may imitate an author's style or form or use a combination of style and form occasionally, but more often, she uses her own individual, unique style, which is illustrated in the following example:

THE DESERTED HOUSE

'Twas once a beautiful abode.
Proud and staunch
And sturdy.
Now the garden walls,
Crumbling and old,
Encircle nothing —
Nothing,
But a tangle of weeds,
Of thorns and brambles;
A few wild flowers.
Nothing remains
But tumbledown ruins
Of the once
Magnificent
Turrets and towers.
The quaint,
Old fashioned windows
Are broken;
Streaked with dust
And rain
As if tears
Shed over memories
Of when the house was alive;

Alive with the merry laughter
Of children
In bygone years.
The flagstone path,
Overgrown with mosses,
Lies untrodden
By human feet.
Birds come
And go, nesting
In the rotting beams,
And in the skylight,
But they never sing.
It seems they know
It's dead;
Cool and quiet
Like a tomb;
The dwelling place
Of silence.

How can you, as a beginning teacher, encourage creativity in hobbies? First of all, hobbies must be encouraged by you, the teacher. Then from the activities, displays, individual or group discussions, hobby shows, or hobby units of study, the student often sees further avenues for adventure in his own particular hobby.

3. Mathematics in High School: High school mathematics offers many opportunities for the student to be creative, if creativity is thought of as activity which is original to the experience of the student.

The teacher of mathematics can encourage creativity on the part of the student by refraining from stereotyping the method of solutions to problems and proofs. A certain minimum amount of form and procedure must be established at the outset of the development of the work. Following this, the student should be encouraged to develop his own techniques.

Hardly a day passes that a student in mathematics will not offer an original proof in geometry or a unique solution in algebra. To illustrate, the following incident was reported recently at a high school faculty meeting:

The class had as an assignment this theorem: THE SUM OF THE ANGLES OF A TRIANGLE IS 180°. In the textbook the proof had been outlined and illustrated with an appropriate figure. After one student had spoken to the class discussing the proof suggested by the textbook author, another student suggested that a different proof was possible. The second student was asked to present his ideas to the class, and it was found that his proof had merit. It also seemed to be more clear for some of his classmates.

It goes without saying that geometry teachers should encourage their classes to look for several ways to prove theorems and exercises. The fact that there is no best way to prove each exercise seems to give each student confidence that his plan, although different, has merit.

REFERENCES

Noy, J. "Youth protest and the age of creativity," *Creative Behavior,* Fall 1970, 4:223-33.

Paffard, M. K. "Creative activities and peak experiences," *British Journal Education Psychology,* November 1970, 40:283-90.

Wood, R. W. "Brainstorming: a creative way to learn," *Education,* November 1970, 91:160-2.

Foster, D. L. "Can creativity be taught?" *Music Journal,* March 1969, 27:36.

Chapter 4

Instructional Planning

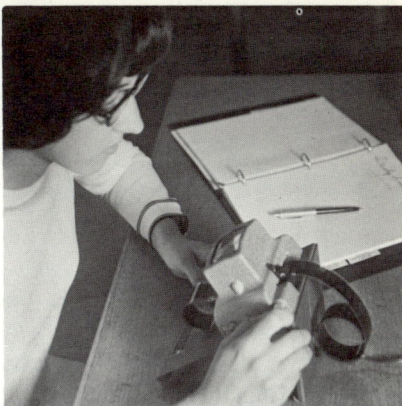

INTRODUCTION

EFFECTIVE TEACHING ALWAYS requires careful planning well in advance of the lesson to be taught. This is as true for the veteran teacher as it is for the novice. As you probably have assumed, the more one teaches successfully, the more one is able to learn short cuts in planning as well as to put less down on an actual paper plan.

Sound planning is particularly important to you as a beginning teacher for the following reasons:

1. It will give you a feeling of security in carrying out your total assignment, and it will help to prevent you from wandering or going astray.

2. It will give purpose to your questions and explanatory helps to the class while aiding you to eliminate useless questions that can consume valuable classroom discussion.

3. It will indicate what is to come next should you become embarrassed or temporarily "thrown off track."

4. It will help give your class a sense of pride and respect for you as a teacher.

THE ACTUAL PLANNING

Generally speaking, there are three types of planning — long-range, unit, and daily lesson planning. Before you can develop any one of these plans effectively, you will need to have the answers to these basic questions:

1. What should the class objectives be — both long term and immediate?

2. What should be the quality and quantity of work expected of the class over a given period of time?

3. What provision can be made for securing instructional materials?

4. What types of learning experiences will be provided for the students?

5. What field trips, if any, need to be provided.

6. Can instructional materials and/or outside speakers enhance the subject matter to be studied?

Planning a series of lessons, like any other type of planning, must be kept flexible to meet emergencies that will arise in the classroom. For example, if you plan to take a vacation motor trip from New York to California, this would be your long-range plan; your unit plan might be certain long segments of your trip covering several days of travel; your daily plan would probably be no more than four or five hundred miles of driving. After careful marking of a detailed road map and taking all the necessary precautions, you would still find need for change all along the way — road repairs, washed-out bridges, short cuts, better alternate roads, etc. Similar conditions develop in teaching a class. Suppose, for example, that you have developed a geography unit on a river system and had planned on using the Mississippi and its tributaries as a case in point. All well and good, until Jack calmly tells you that navigation is his hobby and he has complete charts showing the Amazon River system of South America, which leads Mary to say that she sailed on many miles of the Amazon with her aunt while on a recent South American trip. These comments are followed by much interest and enthusiasm with respect to the new river system on the part of most of the youngsters. Where does this put you as a teacher? Certainly not on the Mississippi, but on the Amazon. This is just one example of an unanticipated change in lesson plans. So that changes can be made on the spur of the moment, the teacher should think out alternate plans in advance of the lesson.

LONG-RANGE PLANNING

As soon as possible, you will want to develop an understanding of exactly what is going to be taught at the time that you begin your teaching experience. If you are a beginning teacher, you know what background your class has experienced since the beginning of the school term. If you are a student teacher, your supervisor can give you an idea of what has happened to date in the educational lives of the students with whom you will be working. You will also want to make use of the cumulative records so that you can understand better the backgrounds — social, economic, and intellectual — of each of your charges. Having grasped an understanding of the backgrounds, you can decide upon the general subject matter to be covered during the course of the school year.

Next comes the division of work. If you are a first-year teacher, you should begin by tentatively outlining the curriculum for the school year with respect to the different units or divisions of work to be undertaken. If you are a student teacher, ask your supervisor to indicate tentatively the units of subject matter and the amount of time to be spent on each. Knowing this, you will want to make plans as soon as possible for getting the job done successfully. Whether you are a first-year teacher or a student teacher, your question at this point might well be: "How much and what length of time should be given to the long-term plan?" There is no rule-of-thumb answer for such a question. Since the largest area of your work is to be planned at this time, a typical outline with a minimum number of subtopics will suffice. Different subject matter and grade areas will affect the quantity involved. After having reached a decision on the question above, you will want to develop your first unit plan.

UNIT PLANNING

Teachers with vision usually organize subject matter around a general theme or center of interest instead of being limited to a chapter-by-chapter development in a single textbook or to slavishly following a course of study. You have probably heard various names attached to this type of procedure, such as centers of interest, units of work, resource units, projects, contracts, problems, and areas of experience. The common term is *unit,* when referring to a main division of the year's activities in which the teacher and the students plan, carry out simple research through instructional materials obtained from many sources, integrate their findings around the general theme, and form their own conclusions and generalizations.

The unit plan of teaching is applicable to any type of school. You can use it effectively to supplement the usual teaching requisites rather than to deter from them. However, there are certain guidelines that you will need to follow before attempting to use the unit approach:

1. Acquire some training for this type of teaching. Some beginning teachers secure their unit training on the job, as it were, becoming successful teachers of the unit approach. Half-hearted attempts at the unit approach by beginning teachers with inadequate background usually produce results far short of those necessary for desirable student progress.

2. Select your topics carefully; otherwise much time will be wasted on unimportant, superfluous, or unsuitable materials for your particular class.

3. Guard against allowing too much freedom in your initial contact with your class. Permissiveness does not mean having children run wild. You must develop effective organization. Good work habits along with desirable attitudes must also be in evidence at all times.

4. Be sure you check constantly the facts and skills being learned by your

students. Using a different method of teaching cannot be made an excuse for the lack of students' learning fundamental facts and skills as specified in the curriculum adopted by the school system in which you teach.

5. Recheck your plans with respect to certain manual activities since they should not monopolize the time needed for the development of skills, concepts, and the correction of faults.

Faced with the demands of a new teaching assignment, you may wonder how one goes about the actual planning of a unit. A few suggestions are provided below:

1. Selecting the Unit. Nothing is quite so challenging and stimulating to a teacher as the tentative selection of the unit of work. Suggested criteria to be applied in selecting from among possible areas of experience follow:

a. Which are most meaningful to the students — most closely related to situations with which they are faced — and which relate to or can be related to their purposes?

b. Which have the richest possibilities in the development of the understandings and skills necessary to cope with life situations for which the school should assume responsibility?

c. Which are best suited to the needs and abilities of the group?

2. Setting Up Objectives. For a teacher to have a successful beginning it is important for him to outline at the outset both student and teacher goals for the unit. The basic problems and situations inherent in any unit and the understandings and skills needed to cope with them must be built into your unit.

3. Developing the Procedure. Browse through available texts, supplementary materials, instructional materials, etc. Determine both kind and number of activities to be incorporated within the unit. This should include the making and using of maps, charts, graphs, models, illustrations, games, dramatizations, etc. Finally, develop your subtopics with respect to available teaching aids.

4. Arranging the Subject Matter. Determine what daily lessons will fit conveniently into your unit. Each daily lesson must be part of the total developmental pattern. If your teaching area lends itself to integration of subject matter, now is the time for you to decide when, how, and to what extent it has a place in the total unit.

5. Teaching the Unit, Making Use of Your Outline Plan. Prepare daily lesson plans as suggested in the following "Daily Lesson Plans."

6. Summarize the Findings. This will be the final development of the unit. The summary should be a brief, cooperative venture developed near the termination of the unit by you and your students. It should imply, as the name suggests, a true, concise summary of the unit study.

7. Evaluation. Did the unit do the original job as you planned it? What were its strong and weak points? If you were reteaching the unit, what changes would you make? Why?

DAILY LESSON PLANS

It is assumed that you now have a general long-term plan organized along with complete plans for the units making up such a total plan. Assuming that you have done a good job of planning thus far, written daily lesson plans are an essential requisite to good teaching. The daily lesson plan should be complete in every detail. It serves the teacher in a student-learning situation much as a house plan serves a contractor in a building project. You will want to write each daily lesson plan in such a way that a smooth transition develops between yesterday's work and tomorrow's work, and it should be in close harmony with both your long-term and unit plans. Although the daily lesson plans should take into consideration the ability, understanding, and background of the class as a whole, you should also plan activities in such a way as to account for individual differences of students found within the class itself.

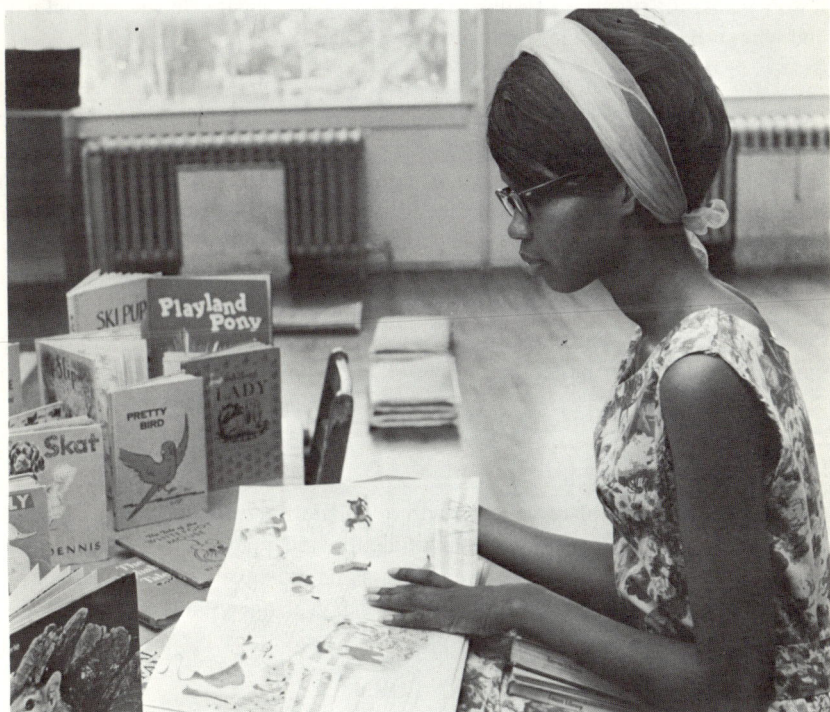

Effective lesson plans provide for a variety of materials for both class instruction and independent study.

Why write a daily lesson plan? No beginning teacher should attempt to teach a class without first having a daily lesson plan written out in detail.

Familiarity with the subject matter *never* compensates for not writing a specific plan. No written plans on the part of the beginning teacher usually "connotes" hearing lessons out of textbooks. Written daily plans will have these advantages for you:

1. Generally speaking, definite commitment to writing induces more specific thinking prior to the actual lesson.

2. A written plan leaves no unforeseen voids and also presents a desirable sequence and continuity of learning.

3. Written statements provide points of reference for the teacher during the actual lesson.

4. What really happened during the lesson? What approach is best for tomorrow? Such questions present no problem to the teacher with well-prepared lesson plans, for notations made after teaching show changes in the original plan and what is best to consider for "tomorrow's plan."

How carefully should the daily lesson plans be followed? Ordinarily, well-prepared lesson plans should be followed rather carefully in actual teaching unless there is some good reason to depart from them. This is generally true with any type of plan. Suppose you plan a motor trip over a certain highway. If you should come to a washed-out bridge you would naturally depart from your original plan. The same idea prevails in teaching. In fact, you should be prepared if necessary to slightly alter or make modifications in your plans as you are in the process of teaching. In other words, take your cues from the students. "Read" them and their reactions to your presentation and make appropriate modifications in your basic plan. Above all, a lesson plan should never become a "crutch." At best it is a means to an end, not the end itself.

DAILY LESSON PLAN FORM

Forms for lesson plans will vary with the materials being taught, the subject matter pursued, the maturity of the students, and your ideas and skills as a teacher. The following form is given only as an example. It should serve as a pattern, help you understand better day-by-day planning, and give you ideas necessary for developing good lesson plans.

A PROPOSED DAILY LESSON PLAN FORM

NAME OF SCHOOL: _____

NAME OF TEACHER: _____

DATE OF LESSON: _____

SUBJECT TO BE TAUGHT: _____

      or

PHASE IN UNIT DEVELOPMENT: _____

1. Aim(s): Consider your goal(s) as well as the student goal(s) in developing and defining your aim(s). Is it your purpose to teach certain concepts, skills, appreciations, attitudes, subject matter, or review? This part of the plan should be definite and to the point. It need not be too inclusive.

2. Motivation: Here a few general statements will suffice. Indicate the means or devices that you plan to use for the purpose of creating interest. A successful teacher always has a few extra motivation devices "up his sleeve" just in case student interest begins to lag during a lesson period.

3. Procedure: This section requires a rather complete detailed, step-by-step description of just what you plan to do and how you expect it to be completed. You should definitely list all key questions that you plan to ask as well as list all instructional materials that you plan to use. The procedure will vary from day to day with respect to your above stated objective. For example, a recitation period need not be included every day; you may want to spend the period in total or in part on these procedures: recitation, supervised study, meeting of interest groups, reports, planning research in the library, field trips, audiovisual aids, constructive activity, and tests or examinations.

4. Mechanics: If any student help is to be used during the period, determine the exact nature of the assistance needed. Specify the duties of each individual and define the time segment necessary to fulfill them. If the teaching of your subject necessitates a portion of the time being devoted to clean-up, develop correct procedures for the students to complete this task in an expeditious manner. Be sure to plan ample time near the end of the period for proper summary and evaluation of the lesson. If you intend to use audiovisual equipment, find out when it is to be brought to the classroom and determine the correct procedures for its return.

5. Assignment: You will want to write the directions for the assignment as you plan to tell it to the class. Not only should you include the pages in the textbook or source materials, but you should point out topics to be studied, activities to be carried out, and, above all, make absolutely clear *what* you expect of the students. Here again, a good motivating device or two is desirable. Just why should the students become excited about tomorrow's lesson? The answer to this question lies in you and in what you have to say about the lesson.

6. Evaluation: How well did your students obtain the stated aim of the lesson? Write out the steps you plan to take with respect to checking the amount of success you accomplished as the teacher and the amount of learning accomplished by your students. Use each evaluation session as a means of learning better how to improve tomorrow's lesson.

Now that your daily lesson plan is complete, put it into operation. No matter how well your plan looks on paper, it will not teach itself. First of all, you must be a believer in the subject pursued. Secondly, you must put every ounce of your personality into making the lesson an exciting and interesting experience. The students should believe that you enjoy what you are doing and your presentation of your subject should demonstrate this enjoyment.

SPECIFIC EXAMPLES OF PLANNING

Two actual daily lesson plans, developed and taught by two different beginning teachers, are presented to show how mechanical lesson-plan structures are developed into active classroom lessons. The illustrations are taken from two different levels, elementary and senior high.

Third Grade Lesson Plan

Phase of Unit Development: Seed and the Baby Plant.

AIMS —

1. To review and recollect some materials about plants and their needs;

2. To give some knowledge of how plants start from seeds;

3. To introduce the baby plant;

4. To provide some appreciation and interest in plants.

MOTIVATION —

1. Explain that all life depends upon plants, and so there will be no living thing without plants. We depend upon plants for food, clothing, and shelter.

2. Show pictures displayed on bulletin board of plants that provide us with food, clothing, shelter, and beauty.

3. Tell students of a planned field trip to a nearby greenhouse to see plants that have been started from seeds and baby plants.

PROCEDURE —

1. Motivate the class by explaining how all life depends upon plants.

2. Refer to pictures on bulletin board of plants.

3. Review these concepts (place answers on chalkboard).

Positive statements:
a. The four main things needed to make plants grow properly:
    (1) Light
    (2) Water
    (3) Good soil
    (4) Air
b. Something happens to plants when they are kept in a dark spot —
    They lose their green color.
c. Plant leaves turn to one side. What causes this?
    Sunlight.
d. Flower pots need holes in the bottom —
    To regulate the water intake.
e. Leaves of plants always go in one direction —
    Up.
f. Roots of plants grow in one direction —
    Down.
g. Something happens to a plant if it gets too much water —
    It sours and dies.
h. Something happens to a plant if it gets too little water —
    It dries and withers.

4. On a chalkboard draw a picture of a seed, the bean, lying open with the protective coat removed and the halves separated revealing the baby plant and the storage place.
a. Discuss the term protective coat and decide that it acted like an overcoat to the baby plant.
Talk about the protective coat of other plants.
    (1) Ones with hard coats like the walnut and the coconut.
    (2) Ones with soft coats like grapes and tomatoes.
b. Discuss the baby plant.
    (1) The part which finally develops into the adult plant.
    (2) The most important part of the seed.
c. Discuss the storage place.
    (1) It provides food for the baby plant during its first weeks of life.
    (2) It shrivels and dies away as the baby plant gets large enough to make its own food.

5. Read and discuss page 25, *The Wonderworld of Science* (supplementary book).

6. Have each student open a lima bean and examine the three parts.
a.   The baby plant.
b.   The storage place.
c.   The protective coat.

7. Have each student take home a lima bean seed to plant. Experiment in classroom:

Planting of seeds in classroom to observe the growth of the bean plants.

MECHANICS —

1. Have all materials ready at the beginning of the class.

2. Materials and other student aids:
a. Pass out supplementary text (end of procedure).
b. Pass out lima bean seed by rows at the end of the period.
c. Collect the supplementary books by passing them forward.
d. Use last five minutes for a summary.
e. Have two children in each row plant a seed for their group.
f. Decide who are to water the seeds and how.

ASSIGNMENT —

1. Tomorrow we will check the seeds we planted in the classroom for any growth.

2. Remind the monitors to water their bean seed, and we will be able to see which group was able to take care of their plant the best.

3. Having first previewed the film ("Planting Our Garden"), prepare class for tomorrow's showing by use of study guide (See Chapter VI, page 113).

EVALUATION —

"An evaluation in checking the amount of success made by the teacher and the amount of learning gained by the students seemed justified by asking questions and receiving answers which were covered in the lesson. I felt that the amount of new material was justified, since all of the students came up to my expectations. I did not secure these kinds of results at the beginning of my initial teaching experience. Sometimes I presented more material than my class was able to comprehend. I believe my success with this lesson was due both to my growth as a teacher and to the constant help I have been receiving from my supervisor. Observation of the students also served as an evaluation and was a clue to the interest that I was able to stimulate."

High School Lesson Plan

Phase of Unit Development: Classification of Equations.

AIMS —

This lesson in second year algebra is the beginning of the study of types of equations as classified by their graphical interpretations. Previously the students have studied the methods for solving simple equations and graphing them. They have also learned to identify algebraic terms and arrange polynomials in descending and ascending powers of the variable.

To begin the study of the recognition of the graphical representation of algebraic equations, it is essential that the student recognize the type of equation that he is graphing.

The specific aims of today's lesson are:

1. To review the concepts of algebraic terms and their degree.

2. To define the degree of an equation.

3. To learn to identify linear equations by the method of establishing the degree of the equation.

MOTIVATION –

1. Explain to the class that a graph is a pictorial or visual representation of the relationship of variables given by an equation.

2. Graph the equations x+y=1 and xy=1 to demonstrate that x+y=1 is a straight line, but xy=1 is not a straight line.

3. Discuss with the class the need for a method of classifying the equation to facilitate the recognition of the relationship of the variables without graphing.

PROCEDURE –

1. Discuss with the class the use that is made of graphs to visualize the curves that correspond to particular equations. "Graphs can show us that as one variable increases or decreases the other variable changes in relationship as prescribed by the equation." Graph the following equations on the board:

   a.   x=y   c.   2x=y
   b.   x=2y   d.   xy=1

2. Each line when graphed will be put on the board, using a different color of chalk. This will aid in distinguishing the lines. A legend for the graphs will be used so the students can identify which equation belongs to which line.

3. Three of the equations were straight lines when graphed but one was a curved line. These equations were in 1a, 1b, and 1c. "Could we find something in common about the equations that were straight lines when graphed?" "How did equation in 1d differ from the other three equations?"

4. "We should see a need for defining an equation which will be a straight line when graphed." Write the following definition on the chalkboard:

DEFINITION –

The *degree of an algebraic term* is the sum of the exponents of all the variables in the term.

5. Write the following algebraic terms on the chalkboard and have the class determine the degree of each term:

a. x^2 (degree of two)

b. xy (degree of two)

c. $3x^2y$ (degree of three)

d. 4x (degree of one)

e. $2x^3yz^2$ (degree of six)

6. "We will now define the degree of an algebraic equation." Write the following definition on the chalkboard:

DEFINITION –

The *degree of an equation* is the same as the degree of the algebraic term with the highest degree in the equation.

7. Write the following equations on the board, having the class determine the degree of each equation:

a. x+y=3 (degree of one)

b. xy+y=2 (degree of two)

c. 2x+y=5 (degree of one)

d. x^2+x=3 (degree of two)

e. x^2+xy+3=0 (degree of two)

f. 3x+5y=7 (degree of one)

8. "We can now recognize when the graph of an equation will be a straight line without graphing the equation." Write the following definition on the board:

DEFINITION –

The *graph of an equation* will be a *straight line* if the equation is of *degree one*. When an equation is of degree one, it is called a linear equation.

9. "The exercises on page 52 will aid you in learning to apply the definition for identifying a linear equation. Determine which of the equations are linear. Graph any three of those that you may choose. Determine if the definition is a good one."

10. Ask the class for questions concerning the definitions of any materials discussed today.

11. Write the assignment on the board, and give each student three sheets of graph paper.

12. Give the students a supervised study period for the remainder of the period.

MECHANICS –

1. Have the following materials on hand at the beginning of the class period:

a. White chalk and three different colors of chalk.

b. Clean chalkboard.

c. Perforated board stencil for making graphing grid on the chalkboard.

d. Straight-edge.

e. Graph paper.

2. Take attendance at the beginning of the period and accept entrance slips from those absent yesterday.

3. Check lighting and ventilation of room.

4. Proceed with the discussion as in the "procedure" section.

5. Pass out graph paper after writing the assignment on the chalkboard. Do this by assigning two students to distribute three sheets of graph paper to each student in the class.

ASSIGNMENT –

1. Identify the degree of the 30 equations given on page 52.

2. Graph any three of the equations that you identify as linear.

3. Be prepared tomorrow to defend your decisions as to the degree of the equations.

EVALUATION –

"Through conferences with my department head and review of the current algebra textbooks that are in the classroom library, I became aware of the fact that most textbooks in algebra do not offer a satisfactory motivation for the topic of classification of equations. I was aware that the term 'linear equation' was never too clear to me. I knew that a linear equation when graphed would be a straight line, but how could I recognize a linear equation without graphing it. The books that I examined stated, 'A linear equation contains no exponent higher than one.' How was I going to explain that the equation $xy=1$ was not linear? Surely, these students in second year algebra would challenge me with such a 'loose' definition.

"The conferences with my department head were a great aid. He discussed with me the possibility of writing my own definitions and using them in class.

"The definitions we developed were clear to the class and a good criteria for identifying linear equations. This lesson gave me confidence that the textbook can be improved by testing whether or not the text development is completely clear to me.

"The use of colored chalk to identify different curves that are graphed on the same coordinate axis made it much easier for the class to distinguish which graph we were discussing at any given time. Also, the perforated stencil for making a graphing grid on the chalkboard should be a part of every secondary mathematics classroom.

"The experience that I gained in developing and teaching this lesson has impressed me with the need for giving definitions that are sound and useful. Many of my difficulties in college mathematics could have been avoided by proper definitions when I was a student in high school."

REFERENCES

Monozon, E. and others. "What is the modern lesson like?" *Soviet Education,* January 1968, 10:3-6.

Heese, E. "Do you believe in lesson plans?" *Clearing House,* April 1969, 43:492-3.

Montor, K. "Effect of using self-scoring answer sheet," *Journal of Educational Research,* July 1970, 63:435-7.

Mann, H. "Conducting instruction requires planning," *Teaching Exceptional Children,* Winter 1971, 3:87-91.

Chapter 5

Teaching Techniques

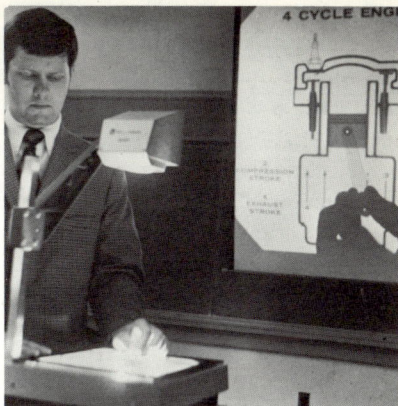

INTRODUCTION

WHEN IT COMES to the application of teaching techniques, almost everyone thinks of himself as a specialist and is ready with advice. Such advice could be sound, but more often it is impractical, false, based on myths or misconceptions, or completely without foundation.

Education is a process of teaching and learning, and it is concerned with the development and growth of young people. In this chapter you will concentrate on one phase of education, namely, teaching techniques. As you probably know, teaching techniques are simply the processes, manipulations, or procedures that teachers use as a means of doing their best job of teaching.

In this age of accelerating change, the teaching profession faces a tremendous challenge. While teaching is the vehicle by which adults assist youth to adjust to the world in which they live with a minimum amount of effort, in order to become a master teacher you need more than an interest in the profession. In addition to having a specific attitude and inclination to teach, along with a rich background of subject matter in special fields, you will need to work hard as a beginning teacher to learn *how* to use skillfully various techniques of teaching to bring about a better type of student learning.

FLEXIBLE SCHEDULING

Sometimes overlooked is the pattern relative to scheduling the most appropriate periods of time for getting the most educational benefits from the techniques employed.

Although scheduling of classes is an administrative function, you, as a beginning teacher, should be able to work within a scheduling framework as practiced in the school in which you teach. Also, even if you are a teacher working in a self-contained classroom, you should be able to discuss intelligently with fellow teachers and administrators various scheduling procedures. Of course, scheduling of any sort should be adjusted to the curriculum and not vice versa.

In most modern school systems, a static schedule, such as the Carnegie unit once used in almost all high schools, has been replaced with creative patterns of scheduling.

Historically speaking, a better way of scheduling was long overdue. With the introduction of technology into the schools, the stress on scholarship following the Sputnik event, the need for better ways of making use of staff time and facilities, a reform scheduling method was inevitable.

What educational criteria are used to bring about change in scheduling? Following are four pertinent ones:

1. All courses do not require one one-hour period per day five days per week. Some courses require longer periods of time; others require periods of shorter duration.

2. Generally, a many-period day creates the necessity for study halls. For many years educators have branded "study halls" inefficient educational evils.

3. A seven-, eight-, or nine-period day allows more curriculum flexibility than a day consisting of more periods of shorter duration.

4. Rigid groupings of 30 to 35 students each period of the day every day of the week make flexible scheduling an impossibility. Also, independent study, large or small groupings, is impossible to conduct under such conditions.

Perhaps you have already found many types of programs designed to provide less rigid schedules. Here are four plans that are much in evidence today:
1. Block scheduling: This type of scheduling affords an option of flexibility within the prescribed block of time. As a case in point, consider a core class of English and Speech scheduled for two periods per day. The teachers have the option of scheduling in accordance with the needs of the students — large group, small group, independent study, lecture, and/or discussion sessions.
2. Rotating schedules: Here periods per day are lengthened, but the number of class meetings per week are reduced. For instance, flexibility is provided by the science class meeting four days per week for eighty minutes each. What would have normally been the fifth period is placed on a rotating schedule. It meets at a different hour four days per week. This leaves the sixth period open for cocurricular activities or other academic courses.
3. Modular scheduling: Here periods are reduced to modules of short duration, such as 20, 40, or 60 minutes. That part of the curriculum requiring longer time is scheduled in multiple modules. Curriculum requirements of minimum time are scheduled for single modules.
4. Combination of existing one-hour periods: Perhaps this is one of the simpler

ways of providing flexible scheduling in a traditional school system. For example, one core class meets two days per week for two one-hour periods and one day a week for a single period.

INDIRECT TEACHING

Recently, many of the forward-looking teacher education institutions have placed a new emphasis on teaching on the elementary and secondary levels. They are training teachers of the future to devote a decreasing amount of time to lecturing or direct teaching. As you know, *direct teaching* relies more on the lecture (teacher-talk) method than on student involvement. Now emphasis is being placed on the use of more *indirect teaching* which places the students in a more active role in the classroom. The indirect approach allows the student to answer questions, formulate ideas, and criticize the ideas of other students in the class. Although more research is needed before sound conclusions can be reached, it now appears, all things being equal, that students exposed to indirect teaching achieve better than those exposed to direct teaching. Also, each teacher needs to evaluate his own teaching results, determining which and how much of the two methods is best for him.

As you practice and gain confidence in your teaching ability, you should make use of the instruments which are geared to the analysis of the teaching act that have been developed in recent years. For example, material is available to help you diagnose the interaction and the effect of nonverbal communication in your classroom. Material on interaction analysis can be secured from the Association for Productive Teaching, Inc., 5408 Chicago Avenue, Minneapolis, Minnesota 55417.[1] These materials help the teacher diagnose the interaction that occurs in the classroom between himself and the students. The 1970 Association for Student Teaching booklet, "Teaching is Communicating: Nonverbal Language in the Classroom" by Charles M. Galloway, gives an excellent resume of the role of nonverbal behavior in the classroom and its significance for the teacher and the student.

THE POISED TEACHER

The successful teacher may be readily identified by his poise and calm confident manner. His every intonation and gesture within the classroom evidences the certainty of action which is a part of him. He always appears to be doing what he knows is just the right thing to do at a given moment. He has the ability to handle any emergency which might arise. The students accept him and — even though his methods may not always coincide with ones used by the teacher across the hall — the class progresses. In Chapter II, "Directing Class Activities," and Chapter VI, "Instructional Materials," planning suggestions will

---

[1] E. Amidon and N.A. Flanders, *The Role of the Teacher in the Classroom.* Minneapolis, Minnesota: The Association for Productive Teaching, 1967.

be found that are basic in the acquisition of poise. The teacher must have routine aspects of the classroom under control as well as possess a thorough knowledge of the subject and how to teach it.

Once the class begins, problems of instruction and techniques arise and call for immediate solutions by the teacher. For the beginning teacher, failure to respond adequately to an initial minor problem can give rise to an avalanche of difficulties that can smother the entire lesson. Most instructional methods, of course, are rather highly specialized. They pertain to techniques of teaching in the elementary grades, in the secondary grades, or in departmentalized classes. For developing certain specialized techniques, you will want to rely heavily upon the advice of your immediate supervisor. There are certain general techniques, however, which every teacher must be aware of and master. These are given specialized attention in the following topics of this chapter.

MOTIVATION

Successful teachers are concerned with what their students do not do, rather than what they do. A basic problem confronting every successful teacher is to get certain students to *care* enough to finish an assignment and be successful in their work rather than to fail. It should be pointed out that only a small percentage of students are indifferent to school and what it stands for. These, however, can constitute major problems. Indifferences are always expressed when students fail to see reasons *why* they should learn. Those who learn willingly without encouragement have inherent interests and are said to be *internally motivated*; those who learn with the aid of teacher-provided incentives are said to be *externally motivated*. The difference between good and poor teaching is usually the result of the difference between teachers who have ability to provide successful incentives as opposed to teachers who cannot or will not provide them.

1. Motivation Requisites: "What are some requisites of motivation?," inquired a beginning teacher of her principal. "Think about it, then let's get together and see what we come up with," said her principal. Here is the sum total of their thinking:

a. Interesting subject matter motivates students. Because the subject matter is interesting to you, this does not mean that it is necessarily interesting to your students.

b. When students see themselves as capable individuals, they are motivated. Your students will have a desire to learn if you present the subject matter on their level — neither talk down nor talk up to them.

c. A secure environment provides an atmosphere for motivating students. For example, you should be aware that your students will make mistakes from time to time. Students should not feel that their mistakes will earn punishment.

d. When students see that they have an opportunity for decision making, they are motivated. Teacher-student planning is your means of accomplishing motivation.

e. Achieving more successes than failures motivates students. Neither you nor your students can develop an interest in a subject if it is expected to become "another failure."

2. *Artificial Stimuli:* You will soon find in your teaching that if work is presented in an interesting manner, students are usually intrinsically motivated, and artificial stimuli, such as incentives, are not needed. (Refer to Chapter VI, "Instructional Materials," for ways and means of making assignments more interesting.) If, on the other hand, you find some students still lack reason to want to learn, incentives are in order. In any event, use them as a means to an end — not an end in themselves. Therefore, no award of much value should ever be used by a teacher as an incentive. To do so usually defeats the learning purpose, and taking its place is the purpose to win, which usually encourages cheating on the part of the students. As a case in point, a high school beginning teacher told recently of her experience where a civic organization sponsored an essay contest on the subject of citizenship in which a $100 prize (incentive) was to be given the winner. Both the civic committee and the high school English teacher were excited about the effect such a contest would have on the improvement of theme writing by the youngsters. Since class time was devoted to the project, every student wrote a theme. Likewise, the large monetary value of the prize caused several youngsters to develop a distorted sense of values. The civic organization dropped the whole thing when it was discovered that wholesale cheating was taking place. Some students were seeking all manners of outside assistance, even to the point of sending manuscripts to professional writers for a complete rewrite. This is a rare example, to be sure. However, the use of prizes and awards is questioned by most master teachers for these reasons:

a. It is difficult to find a prize that has a universal appeal to all students. Group appeal is a prerequisite to any incentive.

b. As in the essay example, the prize rather than the desire to learn becomes the objective.

c. Students soon forget prizes and awards.

d. Prizes are usually artificial, since it is difficult to relate them to the desired activity.

e. It is most difficult to keep the prize from becoming the means to the end.

Since material incentives are frowned upon by most teachers, you will want to develop abstract ones, as you go about planning your work. You will find, as many successful beginning teachers have found before you, that honor rolls, leadership rolls, special privileges, publicity in school and local papers, group approval, and other special types of recognition prove to be ideal abstract incentives.

QUESTIONING

The question-and-answer method of teaching is considered by some educators to be the most effective method at the disposal of the teacher. This belief is especially true if the teacher is well versed in the art of questioning. To formulate stimulating and thought-provoking questions and to be able to answer the questions asked by pupils is, indeed, an art in itself. Cleverly put questions also serve as a means of revealing *what* the children are interested in. Knowing student interest makes it comparatively easy for the resourceful teacher to find appropriate avenues of motivation.

1. The Basic Purpose of Questions: Your first reaction might be that the purpose of questions is to find out how much the students have remembered about the materials they studied. This, of course, is one purpose if used properly. However, the basic purpose is to stimulate your students to *think*. You will frequently find that a puzzling question is a good technique in preparing the class for further study. If presented well, it can arouse curiosity to such an extent as to open a whole new field of investigation.

Through proper use of the questioning technique, you can discover students who are poor readers, limited in vocabulary, lacking in question interpretation, weak in judgment, poor in organizing ideas, and lacking a basic understanding of the subject being pursued. You can discover such student weaknesses better through well-constructed teacher-made tests. (For further explanation, see Chapter IX, "Evaluation.") However, you may be surprised to learn how much of the student's mental processes can be discovered through the use of well-prepared oral questions.

2. What are Desirable Questions? Much material has been written on the art of questioning. Suitable questions can be developed for all practical purposes if they meet the qualifications suggested in the following guidelines:

a. Are they simple? Word the questions within the vocabulary limits of your class. Sixty-four dollar words may be excellently used in writing a college theme, but they are definitely out of place in a freshman algebra class. Remember that unusual or new terms make it impossible for the students to answer your questions adequately.

b. Are they challenging? As previously mentioned, a good question causes young people to think. "Who was the first president of the United States?" is a factual question of memory, which requires no reasoning. This type of question has a place during the review or testing period. However, "In your opinion why do you believe Washington was the best man to serve as the president of the United States?" may stimulate not only the student to further thinking, but the whole class as well.

c. Are they clear? Even though the student does not know the answer, the question should be constructed in such a manner that he understands what is expected of him. For example, "Where is Pike's Peak Mountain located?" is a good question. On the other hand, "Where is the mountain?" is a question that cannot be answered until the students know the name of the mountain referred to.

d. Are they specific? Questions requiring general answers should be avoided. You will find that these kinds of questions tend to cause students to verbalize — talking around the subject without actually saying anything. "What kind of weather did you observe last week?" might bring forth a number of unrelated answers. In a sixth grade social studies class, especially if several weather conditions prevailed and you wanted to discuss the effect of rain and its relationship to a specific situation, you might have said, "What effect did the weather of last week have upon local transportation?"

e. Are they definite? Questions should be stated in such a way as to obtain a one-answer reply. "Who was General Jackson, and what is he noted for?" is actually a question involving two answers. A single question should be stated for each expected answer. Also, questions should not be stated in such a way that they can be answered with a "yes" or "no." "Did Alexander Graham Bell discover the telephone?" is a poorly stated question. A better question might be stated thusly, "Mary, tell us about the discovery of the telephone?"

3. Questions Relative to Research Findings: The results of a sound piece of research done by Aschner and Gallagher[2] several years ago is as practical and meaningful today as it was during the time of its publication. You can become a better teacher by putting their findings into practice. They developed a system containing four categories for thinking about questions. The four categories are: cognitive-memory, convergent, divergent, and evaluative.

a. Cognitive-memory Questions: These questions call for facts or other items which can be recalled. A cognitive-memory question is a narrow question and involves rote memory. Some examples are:

1. What is the largest city in New York State?
2. How did you come to school this morning?
3. Who remembers the name of this picture?
4. Name the ABC countries of South America.

b. Convergent Questions: Questions which call for "the analysis and integration of given or remembered data" are convergent questions. Problem solving and reasoning are often involved in this category. The answers to these questions may be predictable, but convergent questions are always broader than cognitive-memory questions. Whether they are categorized as broad or narrow questions depends on how predictable the responses are. Often, you need to know the background of the students in order to determine whether questions ask for

---

[2] Mary Aschner and James Gallagher, "A Preliminary Report: Analysis of Classroom Interaction," *Merrill-Palmer Quarterly of Behavior and Development,* V.9, July, 1963, pp. 183-194.

reasoning or recall. Some examples of convergent questions are:

1. What is there about the position of New York City that accounts for its importance?

2. Suppose that overnight the school were picked up and moved four blocks away, and you were not told of the move. How could you go about finding it?

3. In what ways is this picture like that one?

4. Why are the ABC countries important in South America?

c. *Divergent Questions:* Questions in this category call for answers which are creative and imaginative, which move into new directions. Here are some divergent questions:

1. How might the lives of the people in New York City be different if the city were located in the torrid zone?

2. Invent some ways for coming to school which haven't yet been invented.

3. If our society put an extremely high value on art and wanted to encourage as many people as possible to be artists, how would our schools be different?

4. In what ways might Argentina, Brazil, and Chile be different if they had been colonized by England?

d. *Evaluative Questions:* These questions deal with "matters of judgment, value and choice." They may be either broad or narrow. "Did you like that story?" is a narrow question. "How did you feel about that story?" is a broad question. Some examples of evaluative questions are:

1. Why would you like to live in New York City? Would you like to live in New York City?

2. What method of transportation would you like to use to come to school?

3. What do you think about this picture? Do you like this picture?

4. What things would you particularly like to visit in Argentina? Would you prefer to be a cowboy or a gaucho?

BEHAVIORISM

As you reflect on your psychology courses, perhaps you recall some of the early behavioral psychologists. Edward L. Thorndike and John B. Watson most likely come to your mind as two of the most influential leaders of the early twentieth century in this particular area of psychology. "Did men such as these actually leave an imprint on the teaching in the school where I am assigned?" Such a question could well be a deep concern of yours. Here are seven clues to help you in identifying teachers employing behavioral psychology techniques; such a teacher will:

1. Present the right stimuli to enable students to give the right answer.

2. Reinforce the right answer several times.

3. Teach students to form correct habits.

4. Present awards for all forms of learning.

5. Prefer objective tests as the best kinds of tests.

6. Consider the teaching environment as not complete without teaching machines.

7. Believe that the curriculum should be selected by the teacher and be teacher-directed for the students.

In short, such terms as "conditioning," "connectionism," and "associations" are trademarks of the teacher employing behavioral psychology techniques.

The theory of behaviorism definitely has a place in the education of today's youth. On the other hand, it should not be considered the only philosophy to be employed in the classroom. In fact, you should not overlook other philosophies or combinations of philosophies that you find most successful to you as a teacher.

INTEGRATION OF LEARNING ACTIVITIES

The degree to which the activity-oriented school has been developed in the American education system varies widely. If you could scan the American educational pattern of teaching in one quick glance, you would find that the development of students' skills, techniques, abilities, and attitudes varies all the way from teaching entirely by subjects to teaching by organizing learning more psychologically through such integrated-learning activities as role playing, simulation, and inquiry.

Stated simply, integrated-learning activities means the development of activities whereby students achieve skills, techniques, knowledges, and attitudes in terms of use with respect to a purposefully planned activity based on a meaningful whole. This is in sharp contrast with learning of facts and skills for the sake of learning alone, usually as isolated knowledge without involving practical implications. Schools wholly employing the first type of learning are usually termed activity-oriented schools; those of the latter type are usually referred to as traditional schools. You will also discover that the basic aim of the activity-oriented school is naturalness and informality, as opposed to formality and artificiality.

It may surprise you to find many so-called "traditional teachers" using activity-oriented school methods in their teaching. As a beginning teacher, you should understand the activity-oriented school theories and learn how far they apply or can be applied to the classroom in which you now teach. As a result of your professional background, you have probably discovered that the *project,* the *problem unit,* the *subject unit,* and the *activity unit* are presented somewhat differently by different authorities. Therefore, the definitions of these terms on pages to follow are expressed according to the school of thought of the authors of this book.

1. The Project: The project method has been in use for many years by most vocational teachers. The term was borrowed from them by general educators and was first recognized, as such, in school programs and plays. It has since been adopted in general classroom teaching, if for no other reason than because of its motivating effectiveness.

The project is a large unit of work of practical and significant value having educational justification. It is characterized by its naturalness in setting and real lifelike manner. The completion of a project may involve social, mental, and/or physical, intellectual, and moral experiences. It is further characterized by many types of student activity; it crosses subject-matter lines; it consists of multisource materials; and it concludes with a number of integrated student experiences. The project method can best be identified in the form of concrete understandings, such as making and equipping a frontier settlement, writing, staging, and presenting an original play, constructing a piece of pottery, etc.

2. The Problem Unit: The problem unit is simply a unit of work built upon a major problem along with related minor problems; the problems are intellectual in nature and may or may not involve concrete activity. The problem unit is further characterized by making use of the inductive method of learning. For example, suppose you were going to teach the western movement; using the problem unit approach, you and your class would begin by developing a series of problem-type questions. A basic question might be worded something like this, "What effect did the western movement have upon the development of the United States?" This question, along with a series of minor questions, would give the class direction in collecting, assembling, and organizing information in developing a unit of work. If you so desire, the unit could be further strengthened concretely by developing a natural westward-movement scene, including covered wagons, oxen, miniature men, children, and women dressed according to the time, etc. From a concrete illustration of this kind, it would be an easy matter for you to encourage your students to develop further questions leading to answers pertaining to the social, political, economic, and military lives of the people during this particular period in history.

3. The Subject Unit: A subject unit is referred to by some educators as the *unit plan.* With this plan of study, a subject is broken up into a number of meaningful units or divisions. Each may or may not be integrated with other subjects. However, each unit is studied as a whole. The subject unit is meaningful and purposeful in nature and lends itself well to dramatic expression by the students. Suppose you were planning to teach *Customs and Traditions of Far Away People,* you would probably soon be developing a series of units, each based upon a different kind of people, such as South Americans, Europeans,

Asiatics, and Africans. In developing these units, you would make use of dramatization to a great extent. At the same time, you would want to allow plenty of class time for the preparation, presentation, and assimilation of additional information gathered by the class.

4. The Activity Unit: The activity unit is truly an integrated type of instruction. It is characterized by the students' studying their social and physical environment from an activity viewpoint. Here is truly an example of how all subjects of the school can be capitalized upon in the learning process — music, social studies, language arts, and art. Where the activity unit is used, class periods and subject lines, as such, are eliminated. In their places, the school day is divided into divisions which lend themselves to the best interest of the class with respect to meaningful learning. To illustrate: if you were planning to teach a *Mexican Unit,* you would probably want a block of time two or more hours in length with certain rest breaks characteristic to the age level of the students involved. During these periods of time, Mexican songs would be studied and sung; Mexican art work would be in the making; and certain dramatizations and theme writing would be developed with respect to information about Mexico gathered from the instructional-materials library. You would carry on all of these activities in terms of a common name or goal decided on at the outset by you and your class.

PROBLEM SOLVING

Uninformed laymen often complain that the schools of today do not teach children to reason. This kind of criticism is simply not true, particularly for the teacher who uses problem solving as one technique of his teaching, since at the outset it requires the students' ability to reason. It should be remembered that problem solving can occur in all subjects and life situations, as well as in the arithmetic or mathematics classes. For example, the fields of social and natural sciences and practical arts afford many opportunities for your students to exercise their reasoning abilities.

You will soon learn, if you have not already discovered it, that the most difficult job of teaching is to create situations which afford young people opportunities to think. This kind of independent thinking can be developed if you, the teacher, will provide problem solving in the curriculum. Provisions should also be made to place much of the responsibility for both planning as well as learning on the students. You should be aware of the fact that one of the most important aspects of problem solving is to afford your students occasions to develop originality and to carry on independent study.

A problem is at hand when a mental or physical difficulty presents itself which demands reflective thinking on the part of the learner and the following characteristics are present:

1. It must deal with practical situations.

2. It must be based on the students' previous experiences.

3. It must be challenging and at the same time be within the mental ability of the learner.

4. It must be understandable and stated in a clear and logical language.

5. It must have value and at the same time hold student interest.

6. It must be definite and kept within the scope of the class.

Problems and projects, even though implied by some teachers to be similar, are entirely different techniques of teaching. *The project* requires the completion of an objective unit of work based on a problem or a series of problems, while *the problem* is solved in thought only. Furthermore, *the project* is definitely a purposeful and constructive activity, embracing both the intellectual and physical problems.

In developing your teaching plans, you will have an opportunity of including many problem-solving situations. Following are just a few school-life and academic problems recently developed by a beginning teacher and his class.

1. What can be done to give the community a better appearance?

2. How shall we raise money in cooperation with the school fund-raising campaign?

3. What kind of auditorium program can we present when it is our turn?

4. Will spaceships soon replace jet liners much as jet liners replaced propeller-driven aircraft?

5. Why did Chicago develop into a larger city than did St. Louis?

6. Can the United States and China live peacefully together, even though each has a vastly different political belief?

THE DEMONSTRATION

All things being equal, the demonstration is as effective a teaching device as is a motion picture or television presentation on a given subject. Since the purpose of a demonstration is to give students an opportunity for making observations through seeing, you will want to use it in reinforcing discussion in a number of classroom activities.

Demonstrations are not limited to courses in science alone. Any number of situations may be visualized by the use of demonstrations, particularly where activities and processes are involved. Generally speaking, demonstrations are of two types:

1. The teacher, students, or both give a particular demonstration with or without the aid of materials or equipment.

2. The students demonstrate a particular subject through the avenue of dramatics.

The former might be illustrated by the physical education teacher showing a correct stance; a typing student showing the correct position at the typewriter; or a home economics teacher showing the proper way to thread a sewing machine. An example of the latter might be the showing by a group of students of the effects of good health and sanitation through dramatics.

To insure enlightening your students rather than confusing them, it is recommended that each demonstration, whether given by yourself or your students, follow these guidelines:

a. Are all of the necessary materials, supplies, etc., in readiness prior to the demonstration?

b. Have you laid a thorough background for the demonstration so that its purpose in relationship to the total unit is understood?

c. Are you certain that the demonstrators understand the step-by-step procedure necessary for a good demonstration? '

d. Are you certain that the demonstrator can make a running commentary explaining exactly and logically what the demonstration is about?

e. Have you previously checked the demonstration so that ample time remains at the end of the period for questions and/or repetition of certain phases of the demonstration?

f. Have you planned for a proper follow-up of the demonstration either in class discussion and/or short tests.

TEAM TEACHING

The modern concept of team teaching had its beginning in the middle of the 1950s. Although it has its backers as well as its debunkers, it is one of the newer educational ideas of merit if facilities, teachers, and students are such as to really give it a chance to succeed. Many of the failures of team teaching can be attributed to poorly constructed educational programs in the first place.

You may well ponder the question: What is team teaching, and how can it help me to become a better teacher? In the first place, team teaching provides school systems with better use of staff, provides varied kinds of student experiences, and provides better use of school facilities. Team teaching is nothing more than three or more teachers of the same subject matter area joining together as a team. Planning, teaching, and evaluation are joint responsibilities. Team teaching provides far more flexibility in that the very nature of the team makes possible large group instruction and small group instruction as well as individual instruction.

1. A Team Teaching Model: There are a number of ways in which a team may be organized in terms of each member's responsibility. The best organization of a team depends upon the philosophy of the team members, nature of the curriculum, methods of presentation, and the facilities available. This way of designing a team and its function is far superior to the administration just assigning, say, three teachers to ninety students, letting the chips fall where they may. One of the authors had the opportunity recently of assisting in developing a team teaching model for a public school as follows:

TEAM TEACHING MODEL

Student unit	120
Teaching unit	7

a. One master teacher. This teacher is in charge of the team. As a team leader she plans, teaches, and evaluates the students jointly with the remainder of the team.

b. Two regular teachers.

c. One teacher aide. This person is not a degreed person. She is a housewife. Her duties are routine in nature, consisting of correcting students' work, checking tests, keeping records, and other nonprofessional tasks designated by the team leader.

d. One clerk. This person also is a nondegreed person. She was required to have a typing background for this particular job on the team. Her duties are clerical in nature, consisting of typing letters to parents as well as typing school reports, cutting stencils for duplication of the teaching assignments, and other clerical work designated by the team leader.

e. Two student teachers. At the time of team organization, a nearby university volunteered two student teachers each semester to become part of the teaching team.

The model above should not be followed slavishly. Both the number and kind of personnel making up a team should be decided entirely on the basis of student interest and need.

2. *The Pros and Cons of Team Teaching:* The following five statements indicate some very strong points in favor of team teaching:

a. A single individual simply does not have the time or the energy to do the amount of research, study, and organization necessary for doing a superior job of teaching every aspect of a unit of work.

b. The organization of a well-prepared team shows much of the professionalism found in a team of medical people in a well-organized hospital.

c. Because the teachers generally give their all, the feeling infects the students as they seem to accept greater and greater responsibility for their own success.

d. The general organization of the team itself dictates when group instruction, either large or small, or individual instruction is for the best interest of the students.

e. Increased enrollment, to a certain degree, is possible without the sacrifice of teaching efficiency.

It goes without saying that there are certain weaknesses in team teaching as indicated in the following three statements:

a. If the team members are selected without much thought about their abilities to work together, educational chaos could quickly develop.

b. Generally, those older teachers who are set in their ways could create a bottleneck if they are assigned to a team rather than having it composed of volunteer teachers.

c. The organization of a team without a complete understanding of each adult's role could lead to negative educational results.

THE ASSIGNMENT

The assignment is a vital part of the lesson in all areas of good teaching. It should never be resolved lightly. Rather, it should be made alive and interesting. Wherever possible, students and their teacher should plan the assignment together. In all cases, the students should understand thoroughly *what* they are expected to do in the assignment and *what* the students' purposes or goals are. If these points are understood by them, it naturally eliminates last-minute instructions by the teacher for the class 'to read certain pages, to work out specified textbook problems, to come to the class the following day prepared to discuss a certain phase of work, etc. Actually, there is no special reason why the assignment need be left to the end of the period. It should be made when the class is ready for it or when the students have progressed to a point where they need to be assigned, or to assign themselves, a new phase of activity to help in achieving the class goal of the lesson.

The students should have an opportunity to do these three things: (1) talk about the assignment; (2) ask questions about its meaning, value, and scope; and (3) suggest modifications that would enhance its significance for them. There should be no doubt about the details of the assignment when it is finally agreed upon. Various means of getting the job done, such as administering duplicated study sheets, assigning specified textbook problems, presenting work outlines to be developed by certain groups, can be used effectively. However, the students must know exactly what is expected of them. You must also exercise care in seeing to it that assignments are actually accomplished. Students need to know that the written part of their assignment will be surveyed by their teacher or classmates, that their reading will be checked or immediately utilized, and that problems worked at home or in supervised study will be checked.

You will find that some of your students will actually need prodding if they are to be kept active in their learning. These students will avoid as much work as you, the teacher, will allow. You actually owe it to this type of student to insist that he do his best and to make it unwise for him to purposely miss any part of his assignment.

In working with these students, provide experiences of a concrete, firsthand nature. These students learn best by handling, manipulating, sensing, feeling, and doing. Learning tasks should be specific and simple; learning goals must be definite, clear-cut, and short-range. They should know precisely what to do and how to do it.

You should recognize that it will be difficult for these students to sense relationships, to make generalizations, or to do inferential thinking. They are more skillful in dealing with "who?," "what?," and "where?" than with "why?" type questions. Set realistic goals for the students and, above all, maintain a patient, encouraging attitude toward *each* of them.

DRILL

A synonym of drill is *practice*. You have probably heard this quotation many times, "Correct practice makes perfect." This little axiom actually governs the teacher as to *when* to use drill in the classroom. It can only be justified when the teacher wishes his students to fix and maintain a skill or a learned association that is meaningful and purposeful. You, as a beginning teacher, should not employ it for the purpose of gaining understanding of facts and information without teaching the meaning of the process as a whole. In other words, the use of drill is simply a means to the end, not the end itself. If you concentrate on the memorization of subject matter rather than upon its use or understanding, you will probably overuse drill in your teaching. For example, some teachers use drill in teaching number combinations apart from giving special attention to the purpose itself. As a result, these teachers usually have disinterested students, coupled with the fact that many seem slow, while others seldom learn their combinations at all. You can probably think of similar situations in the area of your own special teaching field.

The preceding paragraph should not leave the impression that drill is outmoded. In fact, just the opposite is true. You will find that drill is not necessary when students are having trouble with smaller segments of a unit. Drill, for example, serves a very useful purpose in correcting errors in many types of learning situations. In learning to strike "M" instead of "N" on the typewriter, for example, it may be found necessary to give specific drill. It might be said that drill should be used when automatic responses or reactions are necessary for the understanding of large unit activities.

THE REVIEW

You probably recall seeing a particular film several times. The first showing was perhaps interesting, but do you remember that after the second showing you saw scenes and heard lines that you could not recall experiencing the first time? When your students travel with you through a unit, they have similar difficulties, in that they cannot grasp everything during the first time through. Therefore, from time to time, you will want to let them see again old materials for the purpose of gaining new concepts, understandings, meanings, and attitudes.

The review and drill are not one and the same as implied by some. The aim of review is to master facts and skills and at the same time introduce new elements along with the reorganization of thought for a clearer understanding, while the aim of drill is the repetition of facts and skills in the exact form in which they were originally learned. The review, then, may be said to be a broader and more inclusive term than drill. For example, if a class was restudying a list of historical dates once learned through establishing associations with the events to which they properly belong, one of two methods might be used: (1) a drill on the original plan, or (2) a review of the dates with associations of not only the events but noted historical characters of the same period. Therefore, when you assign your class to restudy materials for the purpose of review, you will not want to go over the same material each time in the same way. To do so would cause nothing new to be learned.

In planning a review, you will do well to practice sound teaching procedures, such as:

1. Keeping the total assignment well within the range of the class.

2. Being sure that each student knows exactly what is to be done and how much is expected of him.

3. Varying the procedure from that used in the original study.

Here is a list of suggestive assignments from which you might want to develop your next review:

1. Assign certain students to class reports.

2. Assign the making of charts, graphs, pictures, maps, etc.

3. Show visual materials which should give new slants to the unit.

4. Assign certain objective type questions.

5. Be prepared to answer new questions raised by the class.

6. Assign summarizations to be reported.

7. Assign outlines to be developed.

8. Assign certain unit evaluations to be prepared.

IMPROVED TEACHING VIA VIDEO TAPE EQUIPMENT

Now that you have read about numerous techniques of teaching, how can you gain firsthand knowledge on exactly *how* you look and *how* you sound to the students in your classroom? Presently many schools are investing in video tape equipment which affords the teacher an opportunity of not only hearing but also seeing himself in action. If the school in which you are teaching has video tape equipment, you might want to take advantage of Theodore W. Parsons' *Guided Self-Analysis System for Professional Development: Education Series. Teaching for Inquiry.* The six schedules or guidebooks deal with the following topics: (a) Questioning Strategies; (b) Response Patterns; (c) Teacher Talk Patterns; (d) Teacher-Pupil Talk Patterns; (e) Experience Referents; and (f) Levels of Thinking; they can be purchased by writing to Theodore W. Parsons, 2118 Milvia, Suite 307, Berkeley, California 94700. The authors recommend the system highly for all student teachers and first-year teachers on the job. Proper use of these materials and equipment should help you achieve the status of a master teacher in a shorter period of time than it would take without their use.

REFERENCES

Heinz, C. R., and Verduin, J. R. *Pre-Student Teaching Laboratory Experiences,* Chapter V, "Teaching Techniques to Enhance Behavior," pages 45-49. Dubuque, Iowa: Kendall Hunt Publishing Company, 1970.

Miner, B. "Sociological Background variables affecting school achievement," *Journal of Educational Research,* 1968, 61:372-381.

National Education Association. Research Division. *Ability Grouping.* Research Summary 1968-S3. Washington, D.C.: The Association, 1968.

Strickland, S. P. "Can slum children learn?" *American Education,* July 1971, 7:3-7.

Chapter 6

Instructional
Materials

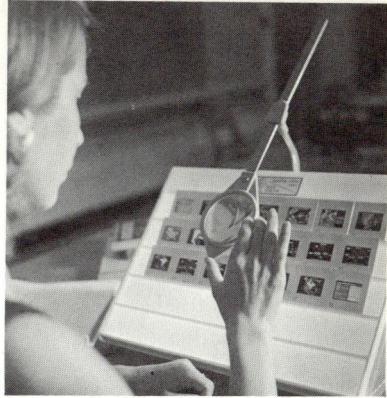

INTRODUCTION

THE INSTRUCTIONAL MATERIALS concept is new and at the same time it is old. It is old because the good teacher has been practicing this concept for a long time; the concept of bringing a variety of materials to the learning situation. The part that is new is bringing together all learning resources which are housed, cataloged, and administered by one staff. Out of the instructional materials concept grew the need for the instructional materials center.

What is the instructional materials center? Some say "it is simply a combination of audiovisual materials and library materials under one roof." Others say "I don't know what it is, but I like the idea that I go only to one place to find all the materials that I need to teach. Not only are they housed there, but they are cataloged in a central catalog so that the finding of materials is simplified." These two statements are mainly teacher oriented. The instructional materials center concept is broader than this; it must take in both the teacher and the student. The student must have all resources at his disposal at all times, imprint materials are not enough. Perhaps the greatest advantage in the instructional materials concept is that it is teacher-student oriented. When the student can use all resources to have a good learning experience, the school then is operating at the proper level of efficiency. The teacher cannot possibly impart to the student all the information that the student now needs. To continue this philosophy is the requirement that the instructional materials center will be opened early in the morning, late in the evening, Saturday, and even on Sunday. Learning then becomes a fifteen-hours-a-day and seven-days-a-week operation.

One of the administration's roles is to recognize that there is *no* need for two separate services, an audiovisual and a library service. The administration should recognize that the importance of all types of instructional materials can better be coordinated by combining the audiovisual and library resources into a single instructional materials center, adequately housed and staffed.

The school administration has concern for at least three aspects of the instructional materials and its center:[1]

1. that the materials acquired and utilized are of the best quality available.

2. that the materials are readily available to teachers and students alike.

3. that the materials are effectively used in the learning process.

The professional instructional materials specialist has the following functions and duties:[1]

1. Consult with teachers regarding the use of a wide range of media in the solution of instructional problems.

2. Supervise the circulation and scheduling of instructional materials and equipment, and the ordering of equipment and materials from sources outside the school.

3. Prepare teaching materials.

4. Assist with selection of equipment and materials, appropriate to the local organization of media services.

5. Provide inservice education for teachers in selection and use of instructional materials and techniques, usually on a person-to-person or small-group basis.

6. Supervise training of students and teachers in operation and use of equipment.

7. Maintain liaison and coordination with district-level media services.

8. Marshal extraschool instructional resources.

9. Help students use the technology of instructional communication.

10. Assist teachers and administrators in evaluating the results of the use of instructional materials and technological resources for teaching.

COMMUNICATION AND THE STUDENT

As a beginning teacher you are first a communicator. Every teacher must be able to communicate with the students, to be a success as a teacher. The dictionary defines communications as "to share in common, to participate in." You must ask yourself:

1. Are the understanding, the concepts, the needs, the goals, etc., that are being presented in your class such that there is a common understanding among the students?

---

[1]*Educational Communication Handbook,* The State Education Department, Albany, New York.

2. Are all the students participating in these learning experiences? If the answer is "yes" to both of these questions, you can be reasonably certain that you are communicating with some of the students.

If your answer is "no" to one or both of these questions, you should examine the way in which materials are being used with your class. You might be guilty of *verbalism.* This is a pitfall many beginning teachers fall into. *Verbalism is the use of words by the teacher that are not understood by the students.* The danger of verbalism is not new; back in the fifteenth century a leading educator was warning the teachers to "Teach things, then words." Only when the student has full meaning of the "things" the teacher is talking about is there communication between teacher and student.

To ensure better communication, present your subject matter materials in an interesting and motivating (study the various ways to motivate as found in Chapter V, "Teaching Techniques") fashion. Use a variety of approaches to the learning situation; students learn in different ways. Here the knowledge of a wide range of instructional materials and the techniques of selection and utilization of these materials will make the difference between a successful or mediocre learning situation.

INSTRUCTIONAL MATERIALS AND THE CURRICULUM

Curriculum is the sum total of those experiences which fall under the direct and indirect supervision of the school. The curriculum is a guide to a well-organized plan of presenting materials to the students in a meaningful and interesting fashion, for the purpose of motivating each student to want to learn.

You should consider the following seven principles in planning the use of instructional materials in the curriculum:

1. Instructional materials should not be separated from the curriculum; they are an integral part of it.

2. There is no set amount of instructional materials that any teacher should use. They are to be used only when there is a need for them and when they will make a unique contribution to the subject matter being taught.

3. Instructional materials provide firsthand and vicarious experiences for the students.

4. When instructional materials are frequently and wisely utilized, they require more work and effort on the part of the teacher, but the results are worth the extra effort expended by the teacher.

5. There are instructional materials available in all areas of the curriculum.

6. The proper use of instructional materials in the curriculum can integrate learning experiences, make these experiences real and meaningful, and thus help to develop well-rounded students.

7. The needs of the student and the curriculum must be the starting point as well as the focal point of all instructional materials in the schools.

LIBRARY AND INSTRUCTION

The library as part of the instructional materials center is used by the teacher and students to locate, gather, and use materials. The library, whether it is decentralized, with a small collection of materials in each room, or in a central location, is the heart of the school. The use of these library materials by the teacher and students will determine, to a large degree, the success or failure of many units of work.

The library should first provide a collection of reference materials on all phases of the curriculum. And, second, it should build up a collection of books for general reading that will appeal to the students of different grade levels as well as different tastes.

Reference Materials

As a beginning teacher you should be familiar with basic reference materials such as encyclopedias, dictionaries, handbooks, and almanacs of various kinds. Only if you are familiar with these books can you guide your students to use them properly.

1. ENCYCLOPEDIAS

Americana: An American encyclopedia, strong in the areas of science, technology, government, and business. Some of the special features are summaries of famous books, texts of documents, excellent maps and illustrations. This encyclopedia is for high school use and is on the approved list in every state.

Britannica: The best known and scholarly of the encyclopedias, oldest now in use. Illustrated with maps in the index volume. Some of the spelling is still British, although it is an American product. This encyclopedia is for high school use and is on the approved list in every state.

Britannica Junior: The subject coverage is broad and keyed to the school curricula, grades 3 through 8. The material presented is accurate and completely reliable at all grade levels. There are illustrations, many in color; maps are distributed through the text. This encyclopedia is on the approved list in every state.

Colliers: A publication which is somewhere between the traditional encyclopedia and the junior encyclopedia. The articles are written in a readable style by authorities in their special fields. The maps and many of the illustrations are in color.

Compton's Pictured: The articles are arranged alphabetically by subjects and there are many illustrations. The articles are planned to meet the curriculum needs from elementary through high school. The reading level of the articles is at the grade level at which the subject matter is taught. This encyclopedia is on the approved list in every state.

2. DICTIONARIES

Abridged Dictionaries

Webster's New Elementary Dictionary, G. & C. Merriam Co., Publisher: Written for students in the fourth, fifth, and sixth grades. Based on recorded works found in books used at this level. 18,000 entries.

Webster's New Secondary School Dictionary: For junior and senior high, with 44,000 entries based on their occurrence in the textbooks and other books used at this level. It has much encyclopedic information: geographical and biographical names, books of the Bible, guides to pronunciation, etc., many illustrations.

Thorndike-Barnhart High School Dictionary: Vocabulary based on the needs of high school students includes biographical and geographical names.

Webster's New Collegiate Dictionary: For college students, with 130,000 entries, emphasis is on the vocabularies of technical and scientific fields. It has much encyclopedic information: gazeteer, vocabulary of rhymes, biographical names, list of colleges and universities in U.S. and Canada, etc., many illustrations.

Unabridged Dictionaries

Funk & Wagnalls New Standard: A one-volume work. It has 450,000 entries. Some of the features are: present-day meaning, spelling and pronunciation, appendix of foreign words and phrases, disputed pronunciation, and population statistics. The modern meaning of a word is given first.

Webster's New International Third Edition: A one-volume work, the best known of the unabridged dictionaries. It has over 450,000 entries. The basic aim is to cover the current vocabulary of written and spoken English. Definitions are given in historical order, i.e., the oldest meaning first.

Special Dictionaries

American Thesaurus of Slang: A comprehensive dictionary of slang. It is arranged in groups of words according to the main ideas which they convey.

Dictionary of American English on Historical Principles: This dictionary includes words in current use from the first English-speaking colonist in America to the end of the nineteenth century. It shows the growth and development of words in America.

Roget's International Thesaurus: A complete book of synonyms and antonyms. The words are not arranged alphabetically, but are grouped according to the ideas related.

Webster's Dictionary of Synonyms: Words arranged alphabetically. Synonyms are followed by antonyms, and it has good cross references.

Webster's Geographical Dictionary: Gives more than 40,000 names of places with geographical and historical information and pronunciation. The usual gazeteer information can be found, e.g., locations, area, population, etc.

3. OTHER USEFUL REFERENCE SOURCES

Familiar Quotations: Bartlett, John: This most famous book on quotations was first published in 1855. There are some 20,000 quotations from 2100 authors.

Information Please Almanac: An annual that contains miscellaneous data and information such as: news of the year, maps, all types of statistics, sports, population, etc. New material added each year printed in red ink. A detailed index.

Paperbound Books in Print: A monthly publication with cumulative issues three times a year, lists available paperbacks. The monthly issue presents previews of forthcoming paperback books.

Who's Who in America: Information on living Americans, published every other year, contains materials on the education, position held, published works, etc., of leading people in America.

World Almanac: An annual, one of the best known and most useful of almanacs. Contains information on a wide variety of topics. The index is located in the front of the book.

THE INSTRUCTIONAL MATERIALS CENTER AS AN INFORMATION AND RESOURCE CENTER

When you assign a student to report on a topic, his first question could well be, "Where do I find information on this topic?" There is a logical way for a student to go about his search. The order of his search will not always be the same. There are certain standard references, but the student needs to think along broader lines. There is the whole area of nonbook materials, e.g., films, filmstrips, records, tapes, still pictures, slides, etc., that needs to be searched. The student's research should be on a multimedia basis. Some suggestions are listed below:

1. A good starting place for the student is a general encyclopedia; be sure it is at the reading level of the student.

2. Are there special encyclopedias and reference books devoted to the field in which his topic is located? The bibliography in the general encyclopedia may help.

3. If the topic is a special event, such as a news item that has happened in the past year, he should look in the annuals and supplements put out by the encyclopedias each year. On a news topic, the annual almanac is an excellent source of information.

4. The card catalog of your instructional materials center should be consulted. Here all materials should be catalogued; this is the opportunity to search a wide selection of materials.

5. *The Reader's Guide to Periodicals* or the *Abridged Reader's Guide to*

Periodicals can be used for current happenings. Your instructional materials center retains back issues of magazines for at least five years.

6. Your instructional materials center may have a vertical file of pamphlets, clippings, and pictures, filed alphabetically. Often some of your best information will come from this source.

7. Check the film, filmstrip, and tape catalogs.

CRITERIA FOR SELECTING BOOKS

Books will be an important part of your work for the rest of your life. When you are called on to select books for your classroom reference shelf, for outside reading, or as general textbooks, you should keep the following criteria in mind:

1. If the book is fiction, will the story hold the student's interest? If the book is realistic, does it present a true picture of life in its more wholesome aspects and characters who are real individuals, not undesirable stereotypes? Is the book written in good understandable English?

2. If the book is nonfiction, is the style of writing easy to understand by the group for which it is written? Is the information accurate and up-to-date? Is the treatment unbiased and fair? Does the author make the subject interesting?

3. Does the book meet, in terms of the student, the accepted literary standards of a similar type of literature on an adult level?

4. Do the illustrations meet the ordinary standards of good art work? Do they fit the text? Are they accurate? If imaginative, will they appeal to the student, and will they develop his imagination along desirable lines?

5. Is the format practical as well as pleasing to the eye? Is it suited to the purpose of the book?

SPECIAL STUDY AREAS AND STUDY EQUIPMENT

In many Instructional Materials Centers you will find special study areas and study equipment. These special study areas give the student the opportunity to study by himself or with small groups; some of the special areas are described below.

The individual study carrel has changed the appearance of instructional materials centers. No longer are there just long tables where students study; now they may go to a carrel and have privacy. Many of the carrels are learning stations equipped with television, dial access, and computerized instruction; the carrel could be equipped to use any or all of these innovations.

A carrel equipped with dial access makes it possible for a student to retrieve any number of audio programs by dialing the appropriate index number. This is an excellent way for students to review, catch up on a lesson missed, or just dial music to study by while waiting for the next class. Some schools have their dial access system connected to the local radio station, so that students may listen to radio any time.

Carrels may be designed so that both audio and video signals may be received by dialing the proper index number of the program. They are equipped with small television sets and the sound is listened to with headsets. This type of carrel will see great use in the future when the cartridge electronic video recorder (EVR) is common.

Computer-assisted instruction is in its infancy. When it is perfected and the cost is lower and software is available, the resources of information available to the student will be unlimited. The computer will bring about more self-instruction in our schools. The learning carrel will continue to have an impact on the design of curricula for many years.

With the flood of information available in print form, storage becomes a problem; the second problem is that much of the older materials are no longer available. In order to have this material available for student use, microfilm and microfiche are being used. Microfilm is a document or books reproduced on 16 or 35mm film and read with a microfilm reader. Microfiche is a sheet of 4" x 6" microfilm which can contain up to 60-70 pages on a single sheet of film and is read with a special reader. These two types of reproduction will be used even more in the future, and they save space.

Language laboratories may or may not be a part of the instructional materials center. When language laboratories are not being used for study of a foreign language, they may be used as a listening station for students. A listening station is an individual carrel or similar accommodation, where the student can dial individual programs, or a small group may listen to a common program.

Listening is an important avenue of learning; up to the sixth grade more learning takes place by listening than any other single learning activity.

There may also be a work room in the instructional materials center where students and teachers have an opportunity to produce materials for class presentations. You will find xerox machines, thermofaxes, microfilm reproducers, and other reproducing and copying machines.

Get acquainted with the instructional materials specialist, if there is one, in your school; he is there to help you and your students to increase the productivity of the learning process.

The following bibliographical references will be helpful in the selection of books and other instructional materials for the elementary and secondary levels:

BOOK SELECTION TOOLS

Elementary and Junior High

Basic Book Collection for Elementary Grades, American Library Association. A classified and annotated list of books and magazines, each title graded, kindergarten through eighth grade, prices given.

Children's Catalog and Supplements, H.W. Wilson.
A catalog of over 3300 books, both fiction and nonfiction. Annotations, bibliographic and grade level given for all books. Titles especially recommended are starred.
Basic Book Collection for Junior High Schools, American Library Association.
A classified and annotated list of books and magazines recommended for small and medium-sized junior high libraries.

High Schools

Basic Book Collection for High Schools, American Library Association.
A classified and annotated list of over 1400 books and 70 periodicals, this lists author, title, and subject index.
Senior High School Library Catalog, with Catholic supplement, H.W. Wilson.
A selected catalog of over 4200 books, planned especially for school libraries; this catalog keeps up-to-date by annual supplements.
Gateways to Readable Books, 4th ed. Ruth Strang, Ethylene Phelps and Dorothy Withrow. H.W. Wilson.
An annotated graded list of books in many fields for adolescents who find reading difficult.

OTHER SELECTION TOOLS FOR INSTRUCTIONAL MATERIALS

National Audio Tape Catalog, Department of Audiovisual Instruction.
A catalog of 5000 audio tapes covering a broad spectrum of subject matter areas.
Index to 35mm Educational Filmstrips, National Information Center for Education Media.
A catalog of several thousand filmstrips, by subject, title, and producer.
Index to 16mm Educational Films, National Information Center for Education Media.
A catalog of several thousand educational films, by subject, title and producer.
8mm Film Directory, Comprehensive Service Corporation.
A directory of 8mm films in Standard and Super 8, silent and sound, cartridge or reel-to-reel. Also included is a directory of 8mm projection equipment.
Educators Guide to Free Films, Educators Progress Service.
A catalog of over 4800 free films, available for the asking; this guide is published annually.
Educators Guide to Free Filmstrips, Educators Progress Service.
A catalog of several hundred free filmstrips, which may be used for the asking; this guide is published annually.
The Audiovisual Equipment Directory, National Audiovisual Association.
An annual directory of audiovisual equipment listing such information as specifications, cost, sources of purchase, etc.

Many state universities, school districts, and larger cities have libraries. Write to these sources for their catalogs and loan policy.

AUDIOVISUAL MATERIALS AND EQUIPMENT OF INSTRUCTION

1. Educational Film: There are two sizes of films, the 16mm and the 8mm; they may be silent or sound, black and white or color. The 16mm is the most common; the 8mm is often a single concept film of from one to four minutes in length. If you are using a single concept film, be sure and ask if it is regular or Super 8 and if it is a single concept film or on a regular reel.

The film is a versatile tool. It may be used to introduce, motivate, or summarize a unit of work. Preview the film before you use it with your class. There are films available in all areas of education.

2. Filmstrip: A series of still pictures in a logical order on a 35mm film, either silent or sound, black and white or color. Most filmstrips are silent; the sound filmstrips either have a record or a tape on which the narration is recorded.

In using a silent filmstrip read the captions aloud. The ability to pace a filmstrip to the needs of your class is the main advantage of the silent filmstrips. Preview before using with a class.

3. Slides: The "2 x 2," 35mm color slide is common. Many teachers make their own slides, since they can be produced with any 35mm cameras.

The educational slide is a versatile teaching material, available in a wide range of subjects and relatively inexpensive.

4. Records: Records are recorded at 78, 33 1/3, 45, and 16 2/3 revolutions per minute. Before attempting to play a record, check the label for the proper speed. Failure to do this might ruin the beginning grooves of the record.

Records should be previewed before using with the class. They are available in most subject matter areas.

5. Study Prints and Pictures: Study prints are large reproductions of photographs, illustrations, paintings, and other graphic media. They should be mounted on cardboard so that they are durable and easy to handle.

The still picture is readily available, found in newspapers, magazines, on calendars, etc. Use pictures that *teach;* do not use pictures *just* because they are pretty, attractive, or free.

6. Bulletin Board: A bulletin board is a surface on which materials can be fastened and displayed. The surface may be cork, softwood, pegboard, or any similar material that will hold tacks or bulletin board wax.

The bulletin board should be an integral part of the planning and work in a teaching unit. The boards should be student-teacher planned and display material should be changed often. It is better to leave a bulletin board blank for a few days than to leave a display up too long.

7. Felt or Flannel Board: A felt or flannel board is a flat surface covered with felt, flannel, or suede to which materials backed with sandpaper, cotton, felt, flannel, or suede will adhere. The materials adhere because of the nap of the base material.

The felt or flannel board may be used at all grade levels. It is inexpensive to construct, easy to store, and the materials for its construction may be made by the children. The felt board is used when a temporary display for a class period is needed. If a more permanent display is needed the bulletin board is used.

8. Chalkboard or Blackboard: The chalkboard or blackboard is a permanent colored or black surface that may be written or drawn on with chalk. The chalkboard is used when a writing surface that is easily erased is needed. It is readily available for group or individual instruction.

Be careful about pasting materials on the chalkboard since the surface may be marred. When using the chalkboard write large; if your writing is poor, then print, for printing is easier to read than handwriting.

9. Radio: Radio is being used in instruction today. Many local school systems have their own F.M. station. Explore the extent to which radio programs are available in your subject matter area. Radio is used to acquaint students with current and "on the spot" events and happenings. Educational F.M. radio will be playing an increasingly important role in the future. The tape recorder has made it possible to tape the radio programs to meet your class schedule.

10. Television: Television for use in the classroom may be open circuit or closed circuit. Open circuit means that the television signal is sent out over the air and picked up by your school with an antenna. Closed circuit is when the television camera and television set are connected by a coaxial cable.

Does your area have an educational television station? If it does, what programs are being broadcast that may be of interest to you? What time are the programs broadcast? Your school may be one of the cooperating schools, or may subscribe to the services of the television station. If it does, you will be able to receive study materials to supplement the aired programs. The use of educational television continues to grow each year.

A closed circuit television system has many uses in schools. It is used by the chemistry students to record demonstrations, for students in speech to study their delivery and facial expressions. In football the coach uses it to study when plays do and do not work. The uses to which this system can be put are endless. An important component of closed circuit television is the Video Tape Recorder, commonly called a VTR. With a VTR it is possible to have instantaneous replay of the audio and video signals from a television system and the tapes may be saved for future use.

A new development in electronic recording is the electronic video recording (EVR) cartridge. This turns the conventional television set into a cartridge-loading projector. The EVR cartridge will play back up to one hour of black and white or one-half hour of color programming. The EVR player is about the size of a small tape recorder and attaches to the aerial terminals of a television receiver.

11. Maps and Globes: Maps and globes are a graphic representation of the earth's surface, either on a flat surface (maps) or as a circle (globe). The globe is the only true map; all other maps are symbolic representations of the earth's surface related on a flat area.

Maps are symbols of reality. The study of maps should begin with simple maps of local areas and expand to more complex maps and larger areas.

12. Charts, Graphs, and Diagrams: Charts, graphs, and diagrams are graphic illustrations which portray ideas by drawings, symbols, or other pictorial representations. They show relationships by means of facts, figures, or statistics and are presented in a symbolic form. In your teaching, make certain that your students are familiar with the symbols used.

13. Tape Recorder: A tape recorder is an electronic means of instantaneous recording and playing back, on magnetic tape, music, speech, and other audio materials. There are two types of tape recorders, the reel and the cassette. The cassette recorder is new. The reel recorder requires that the tape be threaded; with the cassette recorder, the cassette is dropped into the recorder; no threading is required. The cassette recorder is small and portable. Its source of power may be batteries. The sound quality of the reel recorder is superior to that of the cassette recorder. The reel recorder may have three or four tape speeds, such as: 7 1/2, 3 3/4, 1 7/8 and 15/16 inches per second. The cassette recorder usually has only one tape speed.

The tape recorder has many uses in schools such as remedial speech work, developing skills in foreign languages, recording radio programs, recording students' own narration for filmstrips, etc.

Tapes may be erased and used again.

14. Opaque Projector: The opaque projector uses reflected light to project and enlarge opaque objects or material, such as photographs, postcards, written materials, pictures and pages from books upon the screen.

This is a versatile projector. Its main limitations are that it is bulky and the room must be dark to have a brilliant picture.

15. Overhead Projector: The overhead projector operates from the front of the room; the teacher faces the class. It projects transparent materials. This projector will handle transparencies as large as 10" by 10". The projected image appears above and behind the teacher on a screen.

There are many commercially produced transparencies on the market, covering most subject matter taught today. If you wish to make your own transparencies they may be made with a Thermofax, Xerox, or similar machines.

PREPARATION OF TEACHER-STUDENT INSTRUCTIONAL MATERIALS

There will be times when you realize that you are not communicating with the students. You search to find a book, a film, or some material to help you communicate. In this situation you may find the answer lies in preparing your own instructional materials. Some of the areas you may wish to explore are photographic slides, tear-sheets, tape, transparencies, and video tapes.

It is often wise to make this preparation of materials a teacher-student project. One of the best ways to motivate students is to get them involved. The "2 x 2," 35mm color slide is a good place to start. Today, anyone can take good color slides with an automatic camera. If you do not have a camera, check with the Instructional Materials Center; they may have cameras to lend. They will also give you professional advice and help, if you need it.

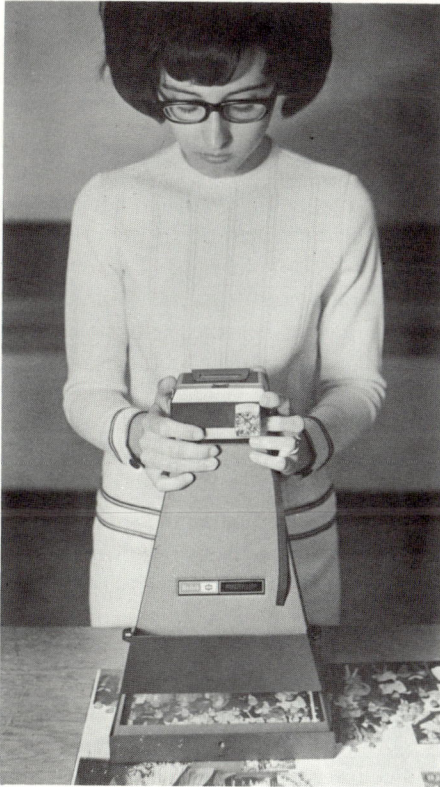

Successful beginning teachers use a variety of tools to communicate with their students.

If there are pictures you need to copy, see if the Instructional Materials Center has a Kodak Ektagraphic camera; this is a copy camera and is easy to use. If you purchase the film, the slides are yours. If the school furnishes the film, the slides belong to the school.

With color film, the film is sent to a processing firm by one of the local photographic stores, and in a week or so the slides are back ready for use. No darkroom or complicated equipment is needed to get started.

Tear-sheets are just what the name implies, pages torn out of magazines and newspapers. There is no better way to make sure that the materials you are presenting are timely than to utilize tear-sheets.

Tear-sheets may be used on your bulletin boards, or be projected with the opaque projector. This material is current and of interest to the student. Not only will you use pictures, but also the maps, charts, diagrams and newspaper clippings. Here are ready-made teaching materials for the taking.

After the materials have been used in class what should you do with them? If the item is such that it will be useful later, put it in your resource file. Some of the materials will be pictures; you may want to copy them on 2" x 2" color slides. Having them on slides enables you to project and blow them up to much larger size than the original. This also preserves them in a durable form.

The tear-sheet can provide the alert and creative teacher with an abundance of instructional materials of very high quality not obtainable from any other source, and they are free for the gathering.

The tape recorder is a versatile machine. There are two basic types, the reel and the cassette loading. Tapes may be erased. This has always been a problem when using the reel type of tape recorder. With the cassette tape, removing the two "U" shape plugs in the back of the cassette makes it impossible to erase the materials. Once materials have been recorded they are permanent. The cassette tape recorder is new, and because it is small and operates from batteries, it can become an individual tutor for the slow and the gifted student.

As a teacher you will be looking for resource people in your community. When they visit your classroom, record them, for they may not be able to return another year. If they are not able to come at all, maybe a group of your students can go to them and interview them. The cassette recorders have automatic volume control microphones, so usually a satisfactory recording is made regardless of the operator's experience with the recorder.

The tape recorder is also a tool that should be used in your everyday teaching, e.g., in reading class (students don't believe they read that badly until they hear themselves); in shorthand class, so that all classes hear the same dictation, or have others (such as businessmen) dictate, so that the students get used to taking shorthand from all types of voices. The list can be endless – the only limitation is that of your imagination to innovate new uses for the tape recorder.

The overhead projector is used more today in the classroom than ever before. Part of this popularity is because teachers find it adaptable to most teaching situations. Teachers are creative people. Another factor is that this type of projector is easily adapted to student projects. The transparencies used on overhead projectors are usually 10 inches square. They may be made with the Thermofax, Xerox, and Technifax processes. Students can also make their own materials for class reports, and it is a good idea to give them an opportunity to use the overhead projector and other media when presenting their reports and projects. They will then be less nervous about getting up in front of their peers, for they feel that the class is looking at the materials and not at them.

Ask if your school has a "primary typewriter"; this is a typewriter with extremely large type. It makes the preparation of transparencies much simpler.

The VTR (video tape recorder), an electronic device that makes it possible to instantaneously replay the audio and video signals from a television system, has already been mentioned.

This may be the replay of a laboratory experiment just finished by your class or of a football play by the coach during practice or an off-the-air recording of a television program to be used later.

Many of the VTR's are portable; this increases the possibility of their utilization. VTR tapes may be replayed many times or stored for future replaying. VTR tapes may be erased and used over.

The VTR has great possibilities when it comes to creating your own instructional materials. There is no waiting for the film to be developed and returned — you see the picture and hear the sound as soon as you replay. The VTR has certainly given the creative teacher a tool with which both he and the students can express themselves with a minimum of trouble.

PRINCIPLES IN THE USE OF INSTRUCTIONAL MATERIALS

When instructional materials are to be used, certain principles should be taken into consideration. If these principles are used, the end result will be more learning by the student.

1. As a teacher you should be thoroughly familiar with any instructional material to which you expect the student to react. When films, filmstrips, records, and other such materials are used, preview the materials before using them. Only then can you be sure that they fit the needs of your class.

2. It is as important to prepare the student for the use of instructional materials, as it is to prepare yourself.

3. When using projected and audio materials, create a learning situation in the classroom that will result in a minimum amount of distraction and a maximum amount of benefit during the actual time when the students are having a learning experience.

4. When using projected and audio materials, check the temperature and ventilation of your classroom. A hot, poorly ventilated classroom is not conducive to learning.

5. Regardless of the instructional materials used — it is important that there grow out of a specific learning situation, learning experiences that are important.

6. Evaluation is the only way of knowing what changes have taken place in your students, as the result of a particular learning experience. Only then do you know whether or not the lesson was effective and worthwhile. You will find a more intensive treatment of evaluation in Chapter IX, "Evaluation."

THE SELECTION AND UTILIZATION OF INSTRUCTIONAL MATERIALS

The selection and utilization of instructional materials may determine the success or failure of your unit of work. Listed below are definite steps that you should follow.

1. The Careful Selection of Materials. There are many sources of materials that you should be acquainted with. Often there are many materials on the same subject. You must evaluate these materials, selecting the one that is best suited to meet the class's needs. You should ask these questions:

a. Will this material make an important contribution?

b. Can the material be used with the room and equipment facilities that are available?

2. The Teacher Preparation. As a beginning teacher you should always preview the material. If it is a film, filmstrip, record, or similar material, a study guide should be used. Research definitely has shown that when study guides are used, more learning takes place. The study guide may be ready-made by the producer of the material, teacher made, or teacher-student made. It is your responsibility as a teacher to plan the class preparation and follow-up so as to achieve the purpose for which the material is being used.

3. The Class Preparation. You, with student help, should discuss with the class the reasons for using a particular material, pointing out the problems that it might help to solve. The concepts the student hopes to gain should be discussed as well as the important points to look and listen for. It is your responsibility as the teacher to establish a proper rapport for the material used.

4. The Showing or Presentation of the Material. The best place to present the materials is in the regular classroom. You should check to see that materials are present. Likewise, check the equipment to see that it is working properly and ready for use. Before class time, you should have the answer to these three questions:

a. Is the room ready?

b. Is the room temperature and ventilation satisfactory?

c. Is the seating arrangement such that all can see and hear?

In a school that has a well-organized instructional program, student operators may do the projecting, relieving the teacher of the task. However, this does not relieve you of your responsibility. Of course, you must know how to operate the equipment because you are responsible for what goes on in the classroom.

5. Application and Follow Up. The discussion of the materials will start with the study guide. The purpose of the guide is to focus attention so that proper understandings, corrections of false impressions, changes in attitudes, and other goals that you hope to achieve are discussed. If there is a need to reshow or replay the audiovisual material, do so. Research shows that more learning takes place on the second presentation than on the first. This rule does not hold for a third showing.

You should discuss with your class what contribution the materials made that was not made in the textbook or from other sources. Questions on these materials should be included in your testing and evaluation of the class. In this way students realize that they are responsible for all materials presented in class.

6. Evaluation by Teacher of Lesson and Method Used. In the final evaluation of the lesson, you should have answers for the following questions:

a. Were the students interested? If not, why not?

b. Has behavior changed? If so, how?

c. Were the goals of the unit achieved? If not, why not?

d. Have the student attitudes changed? If so, were they desirable?

e. Was this the best way to present the materials? If not, how may you improve your next presentation?

As a beginning teacher you will be constantly attempting to improve your instructional ability. Since there is a constant flow of new materials, books, films, filmstrips, tapes, etc., you will need a way to systematically evaluate materials and to keep a record of such evaluations. You should not trust to memory as to whether or not you have previewed a particular material. Actually, the system that you use does not matter very much so long as you keep track of the previewed material. A 5 x 8 inch card is a good size to use for making your evaluation form. It is large enough both to record a great deal of material and to keep from getting lost.

The sample evaluation form on page 79 is a multi-purpose form, and it is mainly for use with audiovisual materials. You may wish to design one slightly different so as to fit your own needs.

INSTRUCTIONAL MATERIALS STUDY GUIDE

It is critical that you prepare yourself and your class before materials are used. One of the common ways is to prepare a study guide before the materials are used. This is an effective way to teach. The class goes over the study guide before the materials are used, then they know what to look or listen for; this is a self starter for discussion. A sample Social Studies study guide given for the film "Colonial Children."

INSTRUCTIONAL MATERIALS STUDY GUIDE

Look For the Answers to these Questions

1. How can you compare the kinds of clothing worn today with those worn in colonial times?

2. What foods did the colonists have? How did they obtain them?

3. In what ways were colonial homes *different* from your homes?

4. What were some of the jobs of the colonial boys and girls?

5. Why did the colonial families have to help each other?

6. What schooling did the colonial children have?

7. What ways did they have to entertain themselves?

Vocabulary

bucket	reward	splint broom
colony	sampler	sweetmeats
gourd	Scriptures	trenchers
hand loom	shillings	warming pans
musket	silversmith	wooden yoke
pence	tallow	

Find These Places On A Map

Boston   Massachusetts   New England States

Some Other Activities For You:

1. Read stories about colonial life.

2. If any of you have colonial articles at home, perhaps your parents would let you bring them to school to show the other students.

3. Would you like to work on colonial handicraft projects such as weaving, spinning, dyeing, candle making, whittling, and so on?

4. If you have hot lunches in your school, perhaps you could request the preparation of a colonial meal.

5. You and your classmates might prepare drawings, written or oral discussions, poems, stories, or dramatizations based on suggested subjects in the film.

INSTRUCTIONAL MATERIALS EVALUATION FORM

Date of evaluation _____

TITLE _____

Film _____ Reels _____ B & W _____ Color _____ Minutes _____

Filmstrip _____ Frames _____ B & W _____ Color _____ Sd _____ Sil _____

Tape _____ Reel _____ Cassette _____ Minutes _____

Records _____ 78 _____ 45 _____ 33 1/3 _____ Minutes _____

Cost _____ Rental _____ Purchase _____

Source _____

Subject matter field or fields _____

Producer _____

Level _____ P _____ I _____ JH _____ SH _____

Major purposes for which material may be used

	Rating Scale
	High Low
1. _____	1 2 3 4 5
2. _____	1 2 3 4 5
3. _____	1 2 3 4 5
4. _____	1 2 3 4 5

Remarks: (quality of photography, sound, etc.; list new words, questions, etc., that may be asked before using materials, follow-up activities and general theme)

REFERENCES

Katsoff, H. "Photography without a camera," *Media and Methods,* April 1971, 7:50-52.

Hawkins, M. "A model for the effective use of pictures in teaching Social Studies," *Audiovisual Instruction,* April 1971, 16:46-48.

Gerhardt, L. N., M. Singer and D. B. Stava, "Books for Spring," *School Library Journal,* May 1971, 17:42-45.

Cianciolo, P. "To each his own," *Top of the News,* May 1971, 27:406-14.

Chapter 7

Desirable Experiences

INTRODUCTION

THE THOUGHT THAT teachers have many duties unrelated to the classroom never occurs to some beginning teachers before the beginning of their first term of teaching. For example, they know about the English teacher selling tickets at the basketball game. But this is only the beginning of numerous out-of-classroom duties that soon become a part of the beginning teacher's professional career.

Your administrators recognize that your prime concern is with your classroom and its students. However, no beginning teaching assignment is complete without provisions for actual experience and participation in the community as a whole. The school and its students are a part of the community — they cannot become separated. To attempt to do so would be an attempt to defeat the actual premise upon which the American public schools have been built. Therefore, you should study and know your students as individual personalities with respect to their role in the community as well as in the classroom. Knowing their role in a community can best be understood through personal knowledge of the customs, traditions, social, and cultural background of the community. This can best be accomplished through your actual participation within the community itself.

COMMUNITY PARTICIPATION

Whether you are a student teacher or a teacher gaining your first year of teaching experience, live in the community. Good arguments are easily presented, showing that it is cheaper, more convenient, or otherwise better to live at home or on campus and drive to the job. However, the only way for you to have an adequate understanding of the community is to live there. In addition, you should plan to spend most of the weekends in the community. In this way, you will have an opportunity to assist and participate in many community activities such as musicals, debates, home-talent plays, community drives, scout organization, parent-teacher association meetings, church and civic societies, etc.

Gathering first-hand knowledge of the community gives you a better perspective of exactly why and how it functions as well as what it expects of its teachers. For instance, find out what is the community's philosophy of education? It could differ from yours. What is the community's sense of values and limitations held toward academic freedom, i.e., modern or revolutionary ideas? You may or may not agree with what you find, but you will be a better teacher in the classroom for having found out.

Sometimes the role of the beginning teacher in an adult world can be unpleasant, as when proper attention is not given to the mores and expectations of the school and its community. For instance, one male beginning teacher had a field day dating some of the eligible girls in the senior class. His supervisor explained that the community recognizes that some adolescent girls have a platonic love interest in young men teachers. Furthermore, the community looks to the teacher to recognize the love affair for what it is and then quickly dismiss it as an occupational hazard. The teacher took the advice as an interference with his personal freedom, and concluded his remarks to his supervisor by saying, "It is not the community's business or anyone else's *whom* I date, *when* I date, or *why* I date." The situation went from bad to worse for the teacher. A few weeks later he was dismissed from his job "for the best interest of the school."

The second major reason for living where you teach is to know first hand the community resources necessary for good teaching. Knowing professional people, agencies, parks, industries, and other community resources causes teaching to become more interesting, stimulating, and meaningful to your students.

One beginning social studies teacher made a study of community resources located within a radius of 75 miles from the school. Then his first unit of work was selected from one of the following classifications:

POSSIBLE CLASS TRIPS AND TOURS

Commercial

1. Post Office
2. Laundry
3. Newspaper
4. Tie Plant
5. Telephone Office
6. Community Deep Freeze

State Parks

1. Pierre Menard Memorial
2. Fort Gage

Industrial

1. Two Coal Mines
2. Glove Factory
3. Pants Factory
4. Ice Plant
5. Oil Fields
6. Tie Plant

Government

1. Court House
2. Mental Institution

3. Fort Kaskaskia
4. Fort Massac
5. National Cemetery

Education

1. State University
2. City Museum
3. City Library
4. Symphony Orchestra
5. Zoo

3. Filtration Plant
4. Fire Department
5. State Penitentiary
6. Federal Penitentiary

Recreational

1. City Park
2. Baseball Park
3. Hockey Arena

Successful field trips, large or small, depend upon advance consideration of mechanics, such as bus fare (if required), lunch, parental permit slip, reservations, and clearance with the proper school administrator.

ADMINISTRATOR'S CONFERENCE

If you are a student teacher, most likely the first contact that you will have with the principal will come when you report to him on the first day of your assignment. Even though you have met him before, report to his office first. He will have been notified of your coming by the college or university, and he will want to become better acquainted with you. Near the close of the visit, he will direct you to your cooperating teacher's classroom.

How many conferences you will have with the principal or superintendent depends primarily on what you want to gain from such conferences. Usually, successful student teachers feel that a minimum of two conferences are needed — one near the beginning of the term and one near the end. Whether you confer with the principal, superintendent, or both depends somewhat upon the purposes you have in mind. The cooperating teacher can best advise you on which administrator to confer with. In any case, remember that administrators are busy people. When you report for a conference, have specific written questions well organized — know exactly what you want to say and why you are there in the first place. The following list of questions seem to be the kind that student teachers usually ask of their administrators during the term:

1. What are some things administrators want to know about first-year teachers?

2. What do administrators look for during their interview with any prospective teacher?

3. What do administrators expect in the way of justifiable reasons for supplies and equipment requests?

4. How much money comes from local sources? State sources? Federal sources?

5. What are some of the things the school and community expect of their teachers?

6. Are rules and regulations governing teachers in printed form? If so, where may I secure a copy?

7. What are my responsibilities as a student teacher? For instance, how much latitude do I have for dealing with discipline conditions?

If you are a first-year teacher, the principal will appreciate your making an appointment to see him whenever the need arises. One of the weaknesses of many beginning teachers, in conferences with their "boss," is that they come literally unprepared. Nothing irks a busy administrator like, "Well I had another question or two to ask, but for the life of me, I can't think of them. Surely they will come to my mind in a few minutes."

The well-organized teacher comes to the administrator's office well prepared. All it takes is a few minutes to jot the questions on "3 x 5" cards prior to the conference. This way you will know what it is you want to talk about. And your administrator will think more of you for it.

STUDENT TEACHER-COOPERATING TEACHER CONFERENCES

One of the more important experiences in the education of the student teacher is the conferences with his cooperating teacher. Effective student teaching can only be had through well-planned conferences. You will find that through conferences you and your cooperating teacher become an effective teaching team developing a respect for and an understanding of the same objectives, methods, and techniques of teaching. This kind of cooperation between the two of you gives the students a sense of security which enables you to teach with a minimum amount of friction or misunderstanding on the part of all concerned.

The conference provides a time in which teachers and student teachers establish common goals. It is a time when the directed teaching experiences can be adapted to fit the individual needs, abilities, and interests of student teachers. It is a time when the progress of children involved can be safeguarded through cooperative analysis of lessons planned and taught. The amount of time, the number of student teachers involved, and the personnel with whom working relations must be established — all help to determine the topics to be included in the conference.

Some of the topics discussed in conference are of a personal nature, such as: evaluating your growth as an individual student teacher; improving your appearance; developing your voice for more effective teaching; budgeting your time for a more effective means of getting the job done; helping you handle classroom problems more effectively; giving you individual academic help when needed; helping you resolve your personal problems more effectively; helping you understand your place in the educational orbit.

KNOW THE NONACADEMIC EMPLOYEES

A nationwide successful superintendent recently made this statement: "One of the most important employees in my school is the janitor." Before you "pooh pooh" this statement think of all the responsibilities of the school that are charged to the janitor. When your list reaches somewhere in the neighborhood of 40 or 50 items, you will begin to realize that the janitor knows something about everything and everybody. In addition, the janitor probably rates only second to the principal in knowing the physical makeup of each teacher in the building. He probably has a better understanding of more students than any single teacher. The reason is obvious. The janitor in his work comes in contact with more students and teachers than any other person with the exception of the principal. Equally important to the school system are the bus drivers, school nurses, cafeteria employees, secretarial staff, school psychologist, etc. Each in his own right contributes far more than you would first suspect toward the successful operation of the school. During the year, become acquainted with these people. Eat in the cafeteria; visit the kitchen; ride the school bus; go on home visits with the school nurse; chat with all nonacademic employees. Have these people tell you about their jobs. Do more listening than talking. The things you learn about the school in general will be well worth your time.

COCURRICULAR STUDENT EXPERIENCES

Most educators agree that the effectiveness of a teacher is determined by his contributions to the total objectives of the school. Although teaching success is due largely to classroom contributions by the teacher, by and large, successful teachers constantly attest to the fact that professional responsibilities extend far beyond the classroom. The modern American schools are complex institutions with many and varied aspects designed for the students. Each one affects their learning and behavioral patterns. Outside the actual classroom itself, one of the most important teacher experiences is the cocurricular program. Every beginning teacher should volunteer to assist in at least one activity, especially if he has previous experience in the area. As a beginning teacher, you should work closely as a sponsor in the field in which you are interested and have special talent. Working with the students in this capacity enables you to provide more opportunities for your students in addition to giving you first-hand experiences in worthwhile professional undertakings. Here are nine benefits to think about:

1. Gives you an opportunity to provide for the development or creation of special student interests.

2. Gives you an opportunity to provide for well-balanced, social, moral, and spiritual student development.

3. Gives you an opportunity to provide for the strengthening of student mental and physical health.

4. Gives you an opportunity to provide for satisfying the gregarious urge of your students.

5. Gives you an opportunity to provide for student school spirit and morale.

6. Gives you an opportunity to develop student citizenship by providing practical experiences in leadership and fellowship through the avenue of cooperation, making use of group and individual action.

7. Gives you an opportunity to provide beyond the classroom for the extension of student creative capacities.

8. Gives you an opportunity to provide experiences in making your students more self-directive.

9. Gives students an opportunity to view your interest in their activities after

classes. Also, it permits them to see you as someone rather than an "8 till 3" teacher.

Most schools provide activities in these fields of interest: clubs (scientific, dramatic, mathematic, radio, television, music, foreign language, etc.), publications (newspapers, yearbooks, handbooks), school parties, home rooms (guidance), student council, outdoor education, etc.

THE TEACHERS' LOUNGE

"Rules, you say, for the teachers' lounge. How ridiculous!" said a beginning teacher to one of the experienced teachers in the new teachers' lounge. Here was a case where an experienced teacher thought she could be helpful by pointing out several customs of the school not found in printed form. Among other things, this school seemed to have an unwritten rule that teachers were supposed to use the lounge only before or after school hours, not during a vacant period. During free periods teachers were expected to remain in their classrooms.

Fortunately, most schools having teacher lounges treat their teachers more humanely than the one in the example above. Generally, there is a room each for the men and women teachers. Just opposite to the example above, most teachers choose their own time to frequent the lounge.

Because, from time to time, administrators, supervisors, school psychologists, as well as teachers, make use of the lounge, many opinions are exchanged between the various personnel. Most likely these people "drop in" for relaxation, coffee, or shop talk. So time spent in the lounge affords the beginning teacher with an opportunity for securing a liberal education.

Many unscheduled experiences are also "cooked up" in the lounge, ranging from the most nonacademic to the most profoundly academic. In one case, many out-of-school hunting and fishing trips originate here. In another case, Pete learns that John is also eating in the school cafeteria today. Since this gives both teachers some free time, they plan together how to make the most of it. Perhaps they will plan a joint teaching assignment.

Generally, much good fellowship and professional understanding are outgrowths of topics of conversation in the lounge.

Here is some food for thought. Teachers, being human, are subject to human error. In rare cases, a few teachers make unreasonable requests of their fellow teachers. And in such cases, the beginning teacher is the number one scapegoat. For instance, a teacher may try to get someone else to do his work. His excuse is that he is busy. More than likely, he is no busier than any other teacher, and someone needs to teach him to do his own work. Usually such bores can be taken care of with the "I'd like to help, but . . ." answer. If he persists time and time again, a more direct answer to the point is necessary. Tell him, for example, that you have all the work you want.

On occasion, the gossip is a source of annoyance in the teachers' lounge.

Sometimes his pitch runs like this: "Oh, have you heard the latest on Superintendent Brown's wife? She . . ." Most likely nothing was heard, but this is a good "pumping" introduction for you to tell something that you heard, if you actually heard anything. The gossipmonger is easily identified as the teacher who is generally talking about everything and everybody. Then, too, this type of teacher soon builds a reputation to the point where other teachers never tell him anything that they would not want to see as headlines in the local newspaper. Whenever you are in doubt about a fellow teacher, the preceding caution is a good order of business.

DAYS ABSENT

Days absent from school might be considered experiences, even though you may think of them as undesirable. For instance, when you are too ill to take care of your classes, no one need tell you "to go to the doctor." But when you cannot come to school for any reason, must someone remind you how to help the substitute?

Actually, you should be prepared for emergencies requiring your absence from school. Here are eight guidelines for doing just that:

1. Keep specific lesson plans easily found by the substitute.

2. Indicate in schedule form out-of-class activities such as field trips, library, assembly, visual aids, and the like.

3. Have textbooks, magazines, supplementary books, etc., easily accessible.

4. Keep your class record book and seating charts in a convenient place.

5. Furnish an assignment sheet, showing exactly what you want assigned. Always supply additional materials so the "eager beavers" will not become problems for the want of something to do.

6. If visual aids or teaching machines are required while you are away, indicate who the operators are and where they can be found. If you ordinarily operate your own machines, be kind enough to secure operators in advance for your substitute if humanly possible.

7. Post fire drill rules and escape routes so both students and the substitute will have no problems in the event of a fire alarm.

8. Indicate how papers, such as tests, examinations, written lesson assignments, are to be checked or graded.

A lot of work for the teacher who is away from her classes? Not necessarily. It is only good practice for a beginning teacher to make specific lesson plans for his own teaching. Most of the other suggestions above can be prepared in a folder labeled "For the Substitute Teacher." This left in a convenient place along with your lesson plans will make for better class adjustment to the substitute during your absence. And your substitute will thank you for it.

PROFESSIONAL EXPERIENCES

One of the quickest ways for a teacher to improve himself and remain successful is to become professionally alive. You will want to become active in as many professional situations as time will permit.

Faculty and small teacher group meetings, such as study groups and committees, provide excellent means for you to know the faculty with respect to how it functions as a unit. Attending and participating in such meetings provides you with answers to questions like these:

1. What is being done in curriculum improvement? Is the newly developed curriculum merely a "boiling down" of a few reference books, or is a definite contribution to the teaching field being pursued?

2. What kind of home-room system is in operation? When did the last revision of the system take place? Who revised it — the teacher or the administrator or both?

3. What kinds of student-progress reports are being used? How long have they been in use? Are they satisfactory to parents, teachers, and students?

Many county and state divisional teacher institutes are open to teachers. Attend and participate in as many of these as possible. Usually your colleagues will be glad to have you accompany them along with other teachers from the same school. Think about the values and contributions such programs make to the teaching profession; listen to and evaluate the reactions from various members of your group.

In addition to teachers' unions and the National Education Association, you will want to become familiar with such organizations as the Association for Supervision and Curriculum Development, the state educational organizations, and professional organizations in your own teaching fields. Study their periodicals and other teaching aids provided by them. Usually the professional library in the school has an ample supply of these materials along with other professional yearbooks, monographs, books, and periodicals.

BEGINNING TEACHER ACTIVITY RECORD

Beginning teacher activities will vary both in type and nature, according to the subject matter taught and the amount of time devoted to classroom, community, and cocurricular activities. You will want to keep a complete record so that you can develop a well-rounded list of teaching experiences as well as having something tangible to evaluate from time to time. The following activity record is a model provided for your convenience in recording your own experiences:

BEGINNING TEACHER ACTIVITY RECORD

Name _____ School _____Year 19_____

Using the topics as a guide, list the experiences which you have had as a beginning teacher. It is a good idea to write the specific things you have learned through each activity and make an attempt to evaluate such learning. Perhaps you will not be able to do everything listed, but use every opportunity that presents itself in making yours a rich set of teaching experiences.

A. In the Classroom

1. Prepare a seating chart and learn the names of the students immediately. Learn more about each student as time moves on.

2. Keep a diary. Use a regular notebook in which you can describe and evaluate what you see and do. Keep it short and to the point.

3. Make and use a specific lesson plan for each day as well as long-range plans. Have these reviewed by your supervisor from time to time.

4. Study and use desirable teaching aids. If you have the ability, construct some of these yourself.

5. Be responsible for a good bulletin board and/or at least one other center of interest in the room.

6. Practice writing on the chalkboard if this is a problem. If your teaching demands drawing figures, such as in science, practice these too.

7. Compile a bibliography of supplementary materials and build a file of your own of such materials. In it include the materials you have used or collected in preparation for your teaching assignment. A steel filing cabinet is ideal for the storage of materials. However, a very inexpensive cardboard filing cabinet may be purchased from your local bookstore. Even a cardboard box serves the purpose very well.

8. Make, administer, and mark a number of tests. Gain all possible experience with standardized tests.

9. Keep a grade book and attendance record. For evaluating purposes, build a file of work done by your students.

10. Take steps to help with the problems of exceptional children, including the gifted, retarded, and ghetto children if they are in attendance.

11. Develop progress charts in skill activities as well as in the other learning areas.

12. Observe and use a variety of techniques such as discussion, drill, recitation, demonstration, supervised study, and team teaching.

13. Plan educational trips with classes and participate in them, observing local school policy.

14. Seek causes for student behavior problems. Make an intense study of at least one case.

15. Have teacher-student discussions. Also, take advantage of informal discussions with students.

16. Observe and apply techniques of opening and dismissing classes in an orderly, but not rigid, manner.

17. Check on the room temperature, humidity, and the lighting situation as well as other physical aspects of the room from time to time.

B. In the Cocurricular Program

18. Assist with at least one cocurricular activity, such as the newspaper, the yearbook, and the various clubs.

19. Help supervise playground, noontime activity, cafeteria, library, or study hall. When needed, take full charge.

20. Find out if certain students have physical or mental handicaps. Some students may be troubled with epilepsy, heart trouble, hearing and seeing problems. Yes, some children even wear dentures.

C. In the School

21. Become acquainted with the work of the school nurse, the guidance counselor, and other agents who work with the students.

22. Attend and participate in all the faculty meetings and general teachers' meetings, including both the County Institute and the State Association Meeting.

23. Attend assemblies, plays, and athletic events. You should assist whenever needed, but make sure to offer help in at least one event.

24. Assist, when possible, with fire drills, nurse's inspection, audiometer tests, speech tests, and other such activities.

25. Have periodic conferences with the school administrators.

26. Speak before assemblies, home rooms, and club groups if invited to do so.

27. Visit other classes and other schools, at every opportunity.

28. Attend and participate in school social functions.

D. In the Community

29. Attend and participate in parent meetings, such as P.T.A.; meet and talk with the parents of the students whom you teach.

30. Arrange for teacher-parent conferences.

31. Visit in the students' homes. Try to get into the home of each parent during the year.

32. Attend community social functions and become acquainted with the townspeople to the extent you have time.

33. Learn the customs, traditions, and pattern of the community and something of the history of the school in which you teach.

34. Learn the philosophy of education in the community as reflected in the history of school referendums, building proposals, etc.

E. In the School Office

35. Become familiar with the plan of the school building. Pay special attention to fire exits.

36. Study the student record system under the supervision of the person in charge. Learn about absence reports and other forms used by the school.

37. Study the philosophy, policies, and objectives of the school. Obtain a handbook if the school has one.

F. In the Profession

38. Participate in informal talks with various teachers about the profession.

39. Become acquainted with a code of ethics, and follow it. (Chapter I)

40. Familiarize yourself with the general magazines in education and with those in your own teaching field. Build a professional library made up of current books dealing with education.

REFERENCES

Norton, M. S. "Know your community in ten easy lessons," *Clearing House,* Summer 1968, 43:55-7.

Stiles, L. J. "School-community information gap," *Journal of Educational Research,* December 1968, 62:inside cover.

Rowley, J. V., and J. B. Galford, "School social events," *Clearing House,* October 1968, 43:110-12.

Thornburn, S. I. "Man who matters (the janitor)" *Times Education* Supervision, January 19, 1970, 2874:34.

Chapter 8

The Beginning Teacher and Human Relations

HUMAN RELATIONS

INTRODUCTION

PERHAPS YOU'VE SEEN him. The teacher who just can't get with it when he comes in contact with people — students, administrators, parents, members of the community. Simply, it boils down to "a reaction." As a beginning teacher, people's reaction to you will go far in having you labeled a success or a failure.

The professional life of a teacher is not much different today from the life of other professional people. Success or failure on the part of the teacher depends primarily on his ability to work and get along with people. This fact is nothing new, for what is now known as "public or human relations" has been understood by all great men of history. The reason that some men succeeded while many other men failed was because the first understood how to get along with people, while the latter often floundered, failing to understand how to acquire good will on the part of their colleagues. You will now have an opportunity to demonstrate your ability to work with and to understand all kinds of people.

Just what is human relations? There are wide and varied concepts of the term "public or human relations." Here is one definition you might want to think about and adopt: *Public relations* is a discovery. It is a discovery of finding out what people like about you and doing more and more of it. Less tasteful but more important, it is finding out what people don't like about you and doing less and less of it.

Since the success of public relations depends upon an understanding of the principles, facts, and concepts of human behavior, the remainder of the chapter will be devoted to these areas. Undoubtedly, you have learned in psychology courses that a knowledge of principles, attitudes, etc., is simply not enough. The ability to verbalize is not always an assurance that the principle of conduct will be translated into desirable action. Knowledge is useful; however, in addition these two things are needed: (1) a desire or wish to change and (2) an atmosphere which will encourage and promote the improvement of present practices.

The following case indicates something about the nature of the reading for the remainder of this chapter:

The principal had just dismissed two of his beginning teachers from a conference.

The conversation between the two beginning teachers as they left the conference room went something on this order:

"What's eating him?"

"He says I was supposed to notify him that a woman representing Mary's mother took her from school at three o'clock this afternoon."

"Well, why didn't you notify him?"

"He never told me to."

Do you recall something similar happening to you? Have you ever been criticized for not reporting something because you were not quite sure it was your job? In other words, were you ever expected to be a "mind reader"?

Many factors are involved in a situation like this. The important point to remember is that things get done through people working together. You will find that each person in your environment has a particular job to do in order to improve the quality of the instruction. Your immediate job, as a beginning teacher, is to discover how you fit into the total educational picture.

Perhaps you will have an early experience in the classroom of helping some of the students become better individuals through working with them. For example, a beginning teacher recently told this story of one of his students:

Glenn D. had a good record in years gone by. His cumulative record showed that he made good grades and was a well-adjusted student. However, there seemed to be a change in Glenn since he returned to school in the fall. Instead of his former cheerful, happy self, he had become quiet and rather sullen in his attitude. Rarely did he smile, and he apparently resented anyone who questioned his authority. He was not a bad boy, but it was getting so that other children resented him. I found that he and I had a common interest. Both of us were interested in stamp collecting. One day while we were comparing a rare stamp from a distant part of the world, I asked him, in a pleasant tone of voice, if anything was bothering him. He began to talk as if he was glad to get something off of his chest. He told me that he had a problem that seemed to defy solution. It seemed that during the summer one of his best friends had committed an act of grand larceny. Glenn knew that any good citizen should report such an act to the authorities; on the other hand, he was faced with the conflict of "turning in" his friend. The situation seemed to become an obsession with Glenn. He found that he could not sleep well; he had to have a light burning during the night; his parents began to ask questions; his close friends wondered what had happened to him. I listened to his complete story as we sat with the stamp-collection box between us. Finally after we had talked about various ways and means of handling the problem, I concluded with this statement: "Now that we have talked this out, Glenn, I know you will know what is the best course of action to take." About two weeks later, we all noticed a change in Glenn. One day after school, he stopped to tell me how things worked out and to thank me from the bottom of his heart for listening to his problem.

Examples like this help to emphasize the importance of "human relations" in the classroom. A knowledge of the principles of human behavior can make you more sensitive to the causes of and the motivation behind your students' actions. By understanding these principles, you can deal more effectively with them.

The answer to human-relations problems is not always as easy as Glenn's. You cannot hope to become an expert counselor of people overnight. In your dealings with children and adults alike, you will find that some people have many things on their minds which they cannot or will not release or confide in others. Some people will simply balk at being guided in what you think is the right direction.

You can help most by looking squarely at a given situation. Gather the facts if you are to understand why one student seems happy in a certain situation while another seems totally unadjusted. For example, the same harmless watersnake connotes danger to one student and love and affection to a biology student who has been taught the true facts about reptiles.

You will need to examine the facts to get at the symptoms, if you are to have any success in understanding the human behavior of the students with whom you come in contact. Having some background in the field of psychology, you should not have too much difficulty. All you need to remember is to recognize *guesses* when they are guesses and *facts* when they are facts.

WHY PEOPLE BEHAVE AS HUMAN BEINGS

Since a teacher cannot carry out his responsibilities except through people, you should thoroughly understand this business of working with people, especially your students. Perhaps you have read Dale Carnegie's book on "How to Win Friends and Influence People." It would be a job well done if you could put into action the knowledge and understanding gained from such a book. This is more true today than at any time in the history of education. When one of the authors of this handbook began his teaching career, his main responsibility was in using techniques of teaching and supervising the mechanical processes of the school. Times are ever changing. Today, the teacher is not only expected to understand the mechanics of the classroom, the school, and the community, but he is required to be a real leader of people. Leadership functions come under your jurisdiction. You will be expected to anticipate and prevent grievances, misunderstandings, antisocial attitudes, and to deal with them effectively if any of them should arise, especially in the classroom.

At your age of maturity, you probably feel that you are a pretty good operator in this business of understanding human nature. For one thing, you probably feel that this is not too big a problem because you yourself are a human being, and you have had a great many working relationships with people. After all, you have observed certain working school situations. So you probably reason further that out of all of your experiences you have built up sound practices of human behavior and you probably pride yourself upon your ability to judge other people rather accurately. Thus far, you have simply applied subjective reasoning to situations involving people and perhaps things have worked out fairly well for you. One of the difficulties with this type of reasoning is that your impressions about people are not always based upon sound reasoning. As previously mentioned, subjective measures have been taken rather than objective evaluation. This leads to many inaccurate and misleading impressions which actually handicap you in working with people. Not only must you become more "open minded" as you attempt to gather information about human beings with whom you come in contact, but also you should not forget the important aspects of human nature with which you are acquainted. For example, you know that many people act as they do because of the "law of self-preservation" or because of certain reputations that they either have or think they have. Sometimes you will simply judge people as if they were exactly like you.

The behavior of the two students mentioned toward the watersnake is understandable. Some students have been trained exactly as you. Therefore, you question the wisdom of the others. To understand why some children accept snakes, you will have to look beyond the immediate behavior itself — this point is explained in the following paragraph. The important point to remember is that you many times judge others by your own set of standards. The fallacy of this belief lies in the fact that frequently you do not know why you accept or do things as you do. Likewise, you will probably not recognize the fact that some of your students live in a different environment, come from a different socioeconomic background, and have different cultures. Often their customs and traditions are also different.

Psychologists have long claimed that behavior is not inherited. It is caused. If you will look for the causes or symptoms of behavior rather than just the immediate behavioral problem, you will be well on the way toward gaining a better understanding of your students. By now you have gathered that several reactions are possible in the case of the snakes. A third might be to kill or destroy them. These things are responsible for one's behavior — STIMULUS, ORGANISM, BEHAVIOR.

Stimuli	Organism	Behavior
1. Snakes	One pupil — hates snakes	Rejects snakes
2. Snakes	Other pupils — like snakes	Accept snakes

Here is an example that a beginning teacher recently gave which illustrates the STIMULUS, ORGANISM, AND BEHAVIOR formula:

A new student was found to be idle before completing his assignment. For example, after completing the first problem in a 10-problem series, he would sit idle until the teacher reminded him to do the next problem. At the end of the first grading period, he was graded low in arithmetic and checked "lazy" on the checklist of his report card. As a result, the parents of the child complained to the superintendent. Following a conference with the student, the teacher, and the parents, it was discovered that the child had been severely reprimanded the previous year for working too fast and "getting ahead of the class." He simply felt that it was to his best advantage to wait after he had completed a minor task until he had received new instructions. A follow-up showed that this student became a good student, had a fine attitude, and was a credit to his class when he actually understood what was expected of him.

This student's behavior, which was first diagnosed as laziness, was caused by his lack of knowledge of what his teachers expected of him. If you are to improve your students' human behavior you must do these three things:

1. Acquire the habit of assuming that all conduct or behavior of your students has a cause or a combination of causes.

2. Conduct an open-minded search for the cause. If you cannot find the cause, do not hesitate to consult with authorities for help.

3. Either remove the cause or causes, or perhaps move the individual out of range of the problem.

1. Behavioral Action Related to Cause: Every teacher must recognize that behind each behavioral action there is a cause. Knowing that there is a cause will many times prevent you from acting hastily or in a fit of temper. Although the cause may be unknown or hidden, it helps to assume that there was a reason for certain behavioral action. Fairness, tolerance, and understanding of pupils can come about only through an appreciation and understanding of the causes leading up to a particular type of behavior in your classroom.

Physiological basis of human behavior should not be overlooked by the teacher. You will want to know all that you can find out about each one of your students from the physiological point of view. Usually this information can be gleaned from the permanent records. Certainly you will accept the idea that a child who has a chronic ailment "ticks" differently from a healthy child. Good lighting, ventilation, and absence of distracting noises are some conditions in which students usually behave favorably. Saying it another way, the students' physical needs, or the fact that they are not satisfied, cause certain behavior problems and consequently affect the students' learning.

Some problems have both physiological and psychological characteristics. For example, accidents on the playground and in shops, tardiness and absenteeism, fatigue (laziness), and attitude toward you and other teachers serve as good examples.

2. Security: Psychologists tell us that security often stands for self-preservation. Perhaps the classroom situation is somewhat different from other life situations, but not too much. A student has security when he is sure of himself – when he succeeds in his undertaking. He feels secure when he is confident that you treat each student fairly.

3. Affection: If your students sense that you have a feeling of affection toward them, they will also feel secure. This applies also to yourself as an individual. When you feel that your immediate supervisor and principal are concerned about you as a person, you have a feeling of security. If you apply the same principle to your students, you will find that they will have the same feeling. Many youngsters show the reaction to absence of affection by throwing temper tantrums. Most mature people soon outgrow this sort of thing. However, it is not surprising to find students of all ages occasionally throwing a temper tantrum through lack of having affection given them.

4. Attention: No one wants to be ignored. Your students are no exception. They would like to have you attracted to them as well as being attracted by their peers. Most human beings have a sense of pride and a preoccupation with themselves. This behavioral pattern demands that others pay attention. It is important for you to divide your attention among your students, being certain that you do not give over-attention to some and neglect others entirely.

5. Independence and Adequacy: It is human nature that all people want to be praised and held in high esteem as well as to have the respect of their colleagues. Your students are no different. Let them know when they are doing a good job. Make it a practice to recognize their work for what it is – their work. By recognizing only the best work in the class, you ignore one of the principles of good human relations. If you are to have a well-adjusted class, it will be necessary for each student to have a feeling of accomplishing something at the end of each school day, regardless of how small the accomplishment may seem to you. Human nature being what it is, your students will feel futile and worthless without some evidence that they are succeeding.

6. Recognition: Achievement and recognition work hand in glove. The logical persons to give recognition to the students' work are yourself and their parents, for the only recognition worth having comes from people who mean something to those being recognized. Your students will not become unduly excited if the "man on the street" recognizes excellency in their work. However, you mean a great deal in the eyes of each youngster. Your word of recognition has tremendous impact upon the type of behavioral pattern that the student displays in your classroom. You should always give recognition when your students do something that deserves it, for it brings encouragement and support.

MECHANICS OF BEHAVIOR

Even though individual differences are found among all of your students, each one has certain psychological needs that to some degree create his particular behavioral pattern. Naturally, each child behaves in a different way, as he seeks to satisfy his own basic wants and urges in the classroom, in the home, and in the community. Each of your students achieves his goal if his behavior results in the satisfaction of his felt needs. Naturally, one's needs or wants are not always satisfied easily. Generally speaking, it is not usually a question of something standing in the way; it is usually a question of how many things are in the way. For example, Johnny could play marbles all day if he were not in school. Here his teachers, his parents, and local laws and customs are standing in his way. You know that a goal can be reached only if the blockings are pushed aside, ignored, or climbed over. From your experience, you further know that there are many ways of meeting adverse conditions — some desirable, others undesirable. A reasonably mature adult usually figures out a sensible approach to the solution of his problems. In the case of Johnny, he might decide to play hooky as a means of reaching his goal. Part of your job, as a teacher, is to help children like Johnny grow into an adult stage. Therefore, you must be prepared to help him and other students to understand what are and what are not acceptable goals as defined by the society of which they are a part.

Students will often react emotionally or unreasonably if the way to achievement of their goals seems to be blocked by an obstacle or series of different obstacles. Having to work under pressure will also cause frustration. Stated simply, this means that if a particular student's needs are not satisfied he is unlikely to reach his goal. A single act of frustration in itself should not cause the teacher to become alarmed. However, if it lasts over a long period of time, year in and year out, the student's behavior will become very difficult to understand and he will soon become a problem child.

1. Regression: Occasionally, the obstacle standing in the way is met by a retreat to a lower level of behavior. This is known as regression. Symptoms are usually identified as when students pout, cry, tell tall tales, or indulge in excessive horseplay and practical joke playing. This type of behavior, of course, does nothing to actually overcome the obstacles standing in the way of success or accomplishing true goals.

2. Resignation: Another type of frustration behavior is called resignation. In this case, the child develops the idea of "why work anyway? I can't win; study just enough to get by or barely to pass; perhaps play hooky a few times and let come what may." An occasional adverse act is nothing to worry about. However, if this sort of thing persists, you will need to give attention to the student, helping him remove some of the obstacles that are standing in his way.

3. Rationalization: Students sometimes defend their rash actions by making up excuses or alibis which seem to make good sense, but are not the real reasons for the trouble. For example, Mary might say, " I could make an 'A' in geometry if my mother and father would stay home long enough to help me in the evenings with my homework." Working carefully with Mary, you might find that the real reason for her low grades in geometry are two: first, she is below average in intelligence; secondly, she wastes considerable time during her study periods, particularly the time given over for the study of geometry. Rationalization is usually adopted because of the high opinion people have of themselves.

Thus far, the discussion has been based on negative or frustration behavior. If you recognize the symptoms of frustration behavior, then you can begin to seek the causes. In most cases, you will need to know more about the student than merely his name, or the names of his father and mother. Knowing the whole child and having gained his confidence, you, as a teacher, are in a better position to work effectively with him in the classroom.

By this time you are probably asking the question: "What can I do to improve satisfaction and morale on the part of my students?" First of all, you must recognize the fact that all of your students need to feel secure and independent. Your job is to set up an atmosphere of approval within the classroom. Certainly, you are to tell a student when he is wrong and encourage him to do better things. It is possible for you to disagree with certain students and still be pleasant and fair about how you deal with them.

Students need to know exactly what is expected of them and how you think they are progressing. Remember that if the assignment is clear and not too lengthy for the individual student, there is not much possibility of confusion or uncertainty developing. As changes take place, such as the approach to new problems, you should be sure to explain well in advance exactly what is expected on the part of each student. Remember also that anybody can make assignments; it takes a good teacher to make assignments that present a minimum number of obstacles to the students.

THE BEGINNING TEACHER'S ROLE IN HUMAN RELATIONS

To become a master teacher, keep "tuned in" to the students. Attempt to be constantly aware of their feelings and what is going on in their minds. Although no teacher is always successful in this endeavor, the sincere teacher improves with experience. Also, the most empathetic teacher, even though he is experienced, can be overtired, anxious about something or other, or otherwise preoccupied.

More important, some teachers are chronically "tuned out." They are typically unaware of or grossly misperceive what's going on inside students. Following are two prototypes to recognize so that you can avoid falling into either pattern:

1. The Over-Distracted Teacher: Everything seems to bother this teacher — students looking out the window, students daydreaming, students reading ahead in their books — everything outside of the narrow range of what is expected of the student is considered annoying.

2. The Over-Focused Teacher: Nothing seems to bother this teacher. He is so engrossed in teaching the lesson that he is completely unaware of the students who are sleeping, playing checkers, carving the furniture, or passing notes in the classroom.

The behavior of the teachers in both the above examples has one common feature. They are not empathetic to the needs of their students.

Empathy, warmth, and genuineness are three qualities of human behavior that can help you become a better teacher.

1. *Empathy* is an understanding of the basic feelings and thoughts of other people, and is composed of two basic parts. The first of these is accuracy; the second is depth. You should be accurate in your understanding of others. At the same time you should not only listen in depth to the words of the other person but also attend to his feelings and the thoughts behind his words. In other words, you must not only "tune in," you must also listen to and try to understand the feelings and motivations that are expressed both verbally and nonverbally if you are to be truly empathetic.

Sincerely listening to students is all in the day's work of teaching.

2. *Warmth* is an equally important quality. Warmth is the feeling of nonpossessive, nonjudgmental, nonevaluative regard for another person. To show warmth to others, you accept their behavior not as desirable but as natural and normal considering their given set of perceptions and circumstances. You accept persons for *what they are,* rather than *demand what they should be.*

3. *Genuineness* is the third important quality. Genuineness means that a person is not defensive, is natural, and can be himself. A person who is genuine shows no discrepancy between what he says and what he seems to be expressing. He does not exhibit a somewhat contrived or rehearsed quality or air of professionalism. Rather, he is a person who is freely and deeply himself, with no evidence of defensiveness or the presence of a facade.

REFERENCES

Hubbell, N. S. "It still starts in the classroom," *Today's Education,* December 1968, 57:53-5.

Gordon, R. J. "School news in the local newspaper," *Journal of Educational Research,* May 1968, 61:401-4

Smith, R. S. "Teachers: key to better community relations," *New York State Education,* January 1969, 56:21.

Weiser, M. G. "Teaching and the new morality," *Childhood Education,* Fall 1970, 46:234-8.

Chapter 9

Evaluation

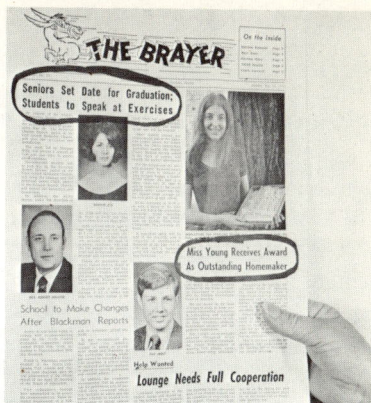

INTRODUCTION

EVALUATION IS THE process of making an appraisal, and it has become a way of life in itself. Hardly a day passes without your making judgments about the value or worth of an object or person. Outside the school, this may be an automobile, a pair of shoes, a neighbor, etc. In school, you constantly judge student progress and achievement; your supervisor, parents, and students make judgments relative to your teaching skills; and you, to become a better teacher, must be concerned with the evaluation of self.

EVALUATION

Evaluation is not something a teacher or a person charged with supervision does sporadically. Rather, it is something that should be done with respect to well-planned objectives or goals.[1] Once these are established, the total process of evaluation is approached from two phases, namely, testing and measuring. The instruments used to measure progress and achievement are commonly referred to as *testing*. The amount or degree of progress and achievement determined is the result of *measuring*.

Testing and measuring are important, but you should not overlook other forms of evaluation. For instance, observation of behavior is a most commonly used evaluation technique. It so happens that attitudes are not measured very well by the use of tests. The beginning teacher, however, can learn to pass judgments on student attitudes by careful observation. Other techniques of evaluation are out-of-class behavior, oral and written reports, group evaluations, and self-evaluations.

---

[1] The objectives for you, as a beginning teacher, are discussed in Chapter I, "Orientation of the Beginning Teacher."

SELF-EVALUATION FOR YOU

You should carefully check your progress at intervals throughout your teaching experience so that you will know how you are improving. It is important that you know which parts of your teaching call for further concentration and improvement and which parts can be continued as you have been doing. You will also want to evaluate your total achievement periodically.

As pointed out previously, the objectives of teaching, which are common to most teaching fields and which you will be concerned with in your evaluation, include those dealing with personal traits and personal growth, control of the learning environment, methods of instruction, subject-matter preparation, relationships with students, community relationships and social reputation, relationships with administration and faculty, and extraclass activities. It should be pointed out, however, that the above areas are not of equal importance to your success. Some have more importance than others to your success as a teacher. However, none are so unimportant that they should be neglected.

General Characteristics: In determining the achievement which you have made in your own personal growth, you will wish to judge such characteristics as dependability, cooperation, and adaptability. You will want to evaluate your leadership qualities, your open-mindedness, and your self-control. Other personal traits which you should check are enthusiasm, ability to express yourself, punctuality, and originality. You will want to check carefully your personal appearance, voice quality, grooming, choice of clothes, and general attractiveness. Ask yourself if you are always well groomed. Are your clothes always neat and clean? Also ask yourself if you have any personal habits which are likely to annoy other people. Do you have any mannerisms which detract from an otherwise good appearance?

Control of Learning Environment: In judging your control of the learning environment, you should check yourself on the attractiveness and orderliness of the classroom and whether you or the students do the greater part of the work to keep it that way. You will want the equipment convenient, properly cared for, and ready for use at all times. Good classroom control will earn for you desirable student behavior which will come without much effort on your part. Ask yourself whether or not the students finish their work on time and leave the room in an orderly manner. Such factors as these will be evidences of your good or poor control of the learning environment.

Teaching Abilities: In previous chapters much discussion was given over to creativity in teaching, instructional planning, teaching techniques, and instructional materials. After each lesson try to decide whether the method which you used achieved desired results. It is not always easy to decide upon the best method to use, but your constant evaluation of the methods which you do use will help you in learning which methods of instruction achieve the best results.

Ask yourself whether you were prepared sufficiently well in subject matter for the lesson or whether there were questions you could not answer and had to evade. The number of questions answered or evaded will give you some index into your own teaching ability or lack of it.

Professional Development: You will wish to check yourself on your relationships with your students. Does a cordial and cooperative feeling prevail or do you antagonize them? Do they avoid you or do they have too much of an attachment to you? Do they talk confidentially with you about some of their problems?

Just as you are concerned with the relationships with your students, you should also be concerned with your relationships with the other teachers, the administration, and the nonteaching personnel. There should be a friendly cooperative feeling at all times. If not, try to analyze the situation to determine the reason. Effort expended now may help you later in securing good relationships with your co-workers.

Each subject matter field has its own extraclass activities closely related to it. You will want to take part in these activities as much as possible. First, participation in activities will help you to learn more about your students than you can in regular classroom teaching; and, second, these activities are the means by which the subject matter may be enriched. In addition to this type of extraclass activity, there are others which are not particularly outgrowths of classroom activity but are of interest to the entire student body, such as athletics, school newspaper, and dance club. You will want to become associated with these. For a more complete treatment read the topic on extraclass activities found in Chapter VII, "Desirable Experiences in Teaching."

Your relationships with the community are other evidences of your qualities as a teacher. Do people in the community respect you? Do they seem interested in you? Most communities are interested in beginning teachers. They are sympathetic toward you and enjoy seeing you succeed. If this sort of relationship does not exist, you ought to try to determine the cause and to remedy it. Ask yourself if your social reputation is good. Sometimes something you have done unwittingly shows up in this manner and prevents your securing good relationships.

Administrator's or Supervisor's Evaluation: In some school systems the principal evaluates his staff, in others a supervisor evaluates them. In still others a combination of educators are responsible for evaluating the teaching staff. Hereafter the word *supervisor* will be used to designate the educator charged with appraising the teaching staff.

Your supervisor is eager to help you become a competent teacher. You will find your relationship with him to be closer than perhaps any relationship you have had with any of your college teachers. Supervisors take tremendous pride in your progress. One of the most effective ways for him to help you is through an evaluation of your work.

A good school system is based upon the premise that the young teacher has reached a certain level of maturity, that he possesses the necessary basic knowledge, that he understands *how* to present his subject, that he has a certain innate teaching ability, and that he not only is interested in teaching but also is interested in becoming a superior teacher. Hence, it remains for your supervisor to discover, by evaluative techniques, your strengths and seek to develop them further; and to discover your weaknesses, where they exist, and seek to overcome them through careful and sympathetic guidance. Your work will become largely a matter of his carefully analyzing your strengths as well as your needs. Following this procedure, he will provide opportunities for you to grow in accordance with the best standards of good teaching and common sense.

For your supervisor to identify your strengths and weaknesses, he must employ evaluative supervisory techniques. The rating scale on page 109, which is representative of the major areas of teacher effort, is suggested as a general guide upon which you will most likely be judged.

Your supervisor's evaluation of you and your work will be continuous. You will learn of his observations primarily in individual conferences. All suggestions, criticisms, and recommendations should be regarded as confidential and taken in a strictly professional way. You have a right to expect criticisms to be given in a kindly, sympathetic, and professional spirit, but with frankness and candor. Your growth should be the highest aim of the conference.

Although educators charged with appraising beginning teachers' work use various techniques of evaluation, the authors feel the beginning teacher is fortunate if he has a supervisor who evaluates through self-evaluation.

To show the effectiveness of self-evaluation, part of a conversation between a principal and one of his beginning teachers follows:

Principal: "John, I would like to talk with you about your science class that I visited yesterday."

Teacher: "O.K. What is it you would like to talk about?"

Principal: "How would you rate yourself on control of the learning environment?"

Teacher: "I believe that I did an excellent job. Actually, I was quite pleased with myself."

Principal: "Did you happen to notice the boy pulling the hair of the girl sitting in front of him? This happened every time you looked at the spectroscope during the demonstration."

Teacher: "Did this happen? I hadn't noticed."

Principal: "What would you say the boy sitting in the last seat in the last row derived from your demonstration?"

Teacher: "Off hand, I'd say that he learned about as much as any other student in the class. I do know that he appeared attentive during the class period."

Principal: "'Appeared attentive,' yes. Attentive, no. Perhaps you failed to notice that his eyes were closed most of the time. At two different intervals, I actually heard him snoring."

TEACHING CHARACTERISTICS

	POOR	BELOW AVERAGE	AVERAGE	ABOVE AVERAGE	SUPERIOR
Check each characteristic as follows:					
GENERAL CHARACTERISTICS					
Cooperation					
Dependability					
Enthusiasm					
Initiative					
Poise					
Appearance					
Voice					
CONTROL OF LEARNING ENVIRONMENT					
Classroom Control					
Handling of Routine Procedures					
Care of Physical Facilities and Equipment					
Attention to Pupil Health and Safety					
TEACHING ABILITIES					
Assessment of Entering Behavior					
Specification of Appropriate Goals					
Knowledge of Subject Matter					
Planning, Preparation, and Use of Varied Materials					
Provision for Individual Differences					
Positive Classroom Climate (Motivation, et al.)					
Use of Varied Instructional Procedures					
Communication Skills					
Evaluation Techniques					
PROFESSIONAL DEVELOPMENT					
Attitude Toward Students					
Ability in Self-Criticism					
Rapport with Fellow Professionals					
Promise of Professional Growth					

Following the discussion of a few more classroom incidents, the teacher was quick to rate himself only "fair" for control of the learning environment.

Next, the principal and teacher discussed various ways of bringing about desirable change that could result in a more favorable learning climate.

Also, during the discussion, the principal was quick to agree with the teacher, as well as to point out why he agreed, regarding situations worthy of excellence.

As the principal took leave, the teacher invited him to "come back anytime for a visit," and the teacher really meant it.

With this kind of teacher-evaluator relationship, the teacher feels comfortable in his job. For he is confident that the evaluator is not only a friend but a professional educator as well — one who is interested in the progress of his teaching staff.

EVALUATION OF STUDENTS

Group Evaluation: It is a sound principle of teaching which holds that learning always begins where the learner's present knowledge leaves off. Failure to observe this principle results in foolish attempts to do two impossible things. One is attempting to teach a student what he already knows; the other is attempting to teach him on a level too far beyond his present knowledge. Both are equally futile. The only adequate safeguard against either of these two situations is in frequent check-ups on the student's success.

In general, of course, education is an individual matter, but schools are broken down into groups or classes. As you know, each school will have established objectives, and within the school each classroom teacher will have more specific objectives which are developed within the framework of the overall school objectives. Schools and teachers must have both types of objectives clearly identified so as to have some direction in which to proceed. The extent to which these purposes are fulfilled depends largely upon the evaluating system in practice. All evaluation, then, should reflect the attainment of some previously defined objectives.

As you make preparations for evaluating the progress of your students, some thought should be directed toward *what* the general group performance will indicate. Since evaluation is a means to an end, you will probably want to improve upon your teaching methods to ensure greater group achievement. This implies, among other things, that you will test not only for retention of subject matter but also for how well other objectives are being achieved. It requires a broad program of evaluation to appraise learning in the many areas involved in the development of attitudes, knowledge and understanding, and functional skills.

Individuals: Your ability to establish effective relationships between your students and yourself will influence how much and how well concepts are learned, understood, and valued. Establishing healthy relationships with boys and girls means knowing them as persons, feeling concern for their problems, and recognizing their interests, aptitudes, and needs. Part of this understanding will come from carefully analyzing test results. Tests should show individuals' strengths and weaknesses and their successes and difficulties. It is not enough for you to stop with the knowledge that an individual made a high or low score by comparison with others. Instead, as you probably believe, a student's curriculum should be based upon his needs and capacities and related to his interests. The more carefully you analyze a student's needs and the causes of his errors, the greater becomes your opportunity to guide and direct his learning and development.

Also, you must be aware that you are testing what *you* have taught. An unusual number of low grades may reflect your poor teaching and/or testing procedures.

Paper and pencil tests are only one way of studying students and of furnishing the information necessary to evaluate the progress they have made toward attaining desired goals. Observations of boys and girls in the daily activities of the educational program will afford you many opportunities to judge the general progress being made. Sociometric techniques may help to throw light on the social and emotional development of your students. Similarly, use aptitude tests, interest and personality inventories, case studies, various kinds of records, including the anecdotal type, along with holding conferences and interviews with students, parents, teachers and other persons such as custodians and other patrons. All of these people have a contribution to make toward evaluating the changes taking place in students.

Teaching your students how to self-evaluate is another technique that should not be overlooked. This technique gives you still another opportunity to learn more about how your students are progressing. Provide periodic opportunities of self-evaluation so your students can learn to develop skills in appraising their own progress and achievement. Rating scales give both you and your students common grounds on which to make judgments. First, have the students complete a self-evaluation instrument. Next, have a follow-up conference, at which time you discuss privately with each student the discrepancies in rating. Do not be surprised if some of your students underrate as well as overrate themselves. Also, do not be surprised if some students hesitate to make a self-evaluation. Many students lack both skill and previous opportunities in self-evaluation.

Since each school situation is different, you should develop a student self-evaluation form based on the objectives as previously planned for your class. A form recently developed by one beginning teacher is given on page 112. You may wish to use it as a guide in the preparation of your own form.

Your ability to evaluate each student's progress accurately is perhaps the most difficult professional assignment you will face. The behavior of boys and girls is highly complicated and is often difficult to understand and interpret.

Objective Measures: It was mentioned earlier in this chapter that an evaluation system should provide for information on students to be gathered from a number of sources. The objective test is only one of the several methods.

In general, teachers have abused this segment of student evaluation by overdoing it. However, there is definitely a place for objective testing in the program.

SELF-EVALUATION FORM

Name of Student _____ Class _____

Place a check (√) following the items to the left in what you consider to be the appropriate square.

	STUDENT'S JUDGMENT					TEACHER'S JUDGMENT				
	EXCELLENT	GOOD	AVERAGE	FAIR	POOR	EXCELLENT	GOOD	AVERAGE	FAIR	POOR
Daily tests and examinations										
Oral reports to class										
Outside readings										
Written assignments										
Contributions in class discussions										
Field trips										
Additional work beyond class assignments										
FINAL GRADE										

An objective test may be defined as an instrument in the scoring of which there is no possibility of showing differences of opinion among various scorers as to whether responses are to be scored right or wrong. It is in direct contrast to a "subjective" test. Usually, objective test items include examples of the following types: completion, true-false, multiple choice, and matching. It must be remembered also that the person preparing these items should follow sound principles of test construction.

Some of the information which you will want to test for can best be done by objective means. You may want to use a standardized test or an objective type teacher-made test. But remember that standardized tests are to be used for the purposes for which they are designed. Your purpose for testing may or may not be met by the use of a standardized instrument.

Each type of teacher-made objective test item has particular strengths and unique weaknesses. For example, the completion type has the obvious advantage of familiarity and naturalness. It is also likely to stimulate desirable study practices and almost eliminates guessing. One weakness is that it tends to measure highly factual knowledge, consisting of isolated bits of information.

Obvious advantages of the true-false test are its apparent ease of construction, applicability to a wide range of subject-matter, objectivity of scoring, and wide sampling of knowledge tested per unit of working time. One of the chief limitations of the true-false test is the factor of guessing. If you use this type test it is recommended that at least 75 items be included. Since test experts have little praise for the true-false type test, a safe rule for you to follow is to restrict the use of true-false tests to those situations in which other types of tests are inapplicable. Having done this, you should give particular care to the wording of the items. Questions should be clearly stated, using vocabulary suited to the grade level being tested.

The multiple choice type item is generally regarded as the most valuable and most generally applicable of all test forms. This is true if unusual care is exercised in its construction. The major cautions you should observe are to avoid irrelevant clues and to ensure that the tests measure something more than the memory of factual knowledge.

The matching test item seems to be well adapted to measuring certain types of learning. It lends itself especially well to the lower elementary grades where students' reading ability is limited. If you are student teaching on this level, you can use the matching item in number work concepts as well as pictures in the areas of social studies, reading comprehension, science, etc. On the higher levels the matching exercise is particularly well adapted to testing the *who, when, what,* and *where* types of situations. To be more specific with the use of matching questions, you may want to use them with events and dates, events and persons, events and places, terms and definitions, foreign words and English equivalents, laws and illustrations, rules and examples, tools and their use, and the like.

The matching test has pronounced limitations. It is not adapted to the measurement of understanding. It has been charged that the matching item is very likely to include irrelevant clues to the correct response. The third major shortcoming is that unless it is skillfully made, it is time consuming for the student.

You may wish to diverge from preparing the traditional type of objective items to which you have been subjected during most of your formal education. It is hoped you are able to modify examples of test techniques which have been reviewed briefly in this chapter. You should also remember that test construction is a highly complicated professional skill — a skill that will require years of experience for the average teacher to master.

Subjective Tests: The most common type of subjective test instrument is known as the essay examination. During the past few years the essay type test has been seriously attacked by professional test experts. Even in the face of the criticism directed against them, essay-type tests probably have a place in a classroom evaluation system and should not be abandoned.

The most popular objections to the essay tests state that they are "commonly or generally employed." These criticisms point out weaknesses in teachers' abilities to construct good essay tests rather than real weaknesses within the tests themselves. Research is conclusive in pointing out that essay examinations as commonly used are weak in the four major test criteria of validity, reliability, objectivity, and usability. Since this seems to be true, it may be worthwhile to review briefly what you can do to ensure better testing by using essay examinations.

You should not feel that it is easier to construct an essay examination than an objective examination. As a matter of fact, it is probably more difficult to construct essay tests of high quality than it is to construct high quality objective tests. Much consideration must be given to their construction, if tests of any kind are to measure anything but mere memory or factual knowledge. Many of the general principles of testing are as applicable to essay tests as to objective tests. So, it seems that essay questions do have a significant place in the school if the questions are well prepared.

You may wish to use one or more of the following words in the preparation of essay examinations: list, outline, describe, contrast, compare, explain, discuss, develop, evaluate or summarize. Remember that the ambiguity and vagueness of essay questions have put this type test into ill repute. Design your questions so the answers do not exceed one or two pages in length. An exception here might well be in the courses of English composition and journalism, where the student's ability to express himself effectively is the major objective of instruction.

Your first concern in a pencil and paper test situation will be to know where and when to use each type of test. This is just as important as it is for you to know *how* to use each type. You must ask yourself "What is to be measured?" and then select either an objective instrument or a subjective instrument, whichever is the most appropriate for the purpose.

Empirical Method: After you have gathered data from various sources which will be of value to you in assigning marks and guiding the future learning of your students, there seems to be one final criterion which you must utilize, namely, an empirical evaluation.

Empirical evidence is the result of personal observation. The final criterion to be employed by you should be that of personal judgment. You will find occasions where elaborately obtained data is difficult to interpret for a number of reasons. In these cases it should be your prerogative to change the student's grade if you are teaching in a system or level where grades are expected.

REPORTING TO PARENTS

For almost a half century, educators have been experimenting with newer and better types of reports from teacher to parent. Many of the changes have been for the better. For example, one such change is to give more information than a "90" or an "A" in a particular subject found on the report.

As a beginning teacher, you cannot and should not attempt to revise the reporting system of the school in which you teach. This is *not* one of the purposes of reporting to parents.

As a beginning teacher, however, you can do much to make current reporting practices even better. For one thing, you can plan to exchange information and advice between yourself and your students' parents. For another thing, you can use the entire marking and reporting system as a means of developing self-evaluation to a point of assisting your students in carrying on self-appraisal and change for improvement. You may choose to report your findings by writing notes and or by holding conferences with the parents. If you write a letter to the parents of each student, include a general summary of his progress with respect to the objectives of your classroom. Always leave the letter open-ended so that the parents feel that you welcome hearing from them and that you value their comments.

Another thought to keep in mind is that both parents and students are given a better idea of student progress if the report makes them aware of exactly what is happening to the student. You can help in this matter, from the student's point of view, by making use of teacher-student planning and regular self-evaluation sessions.

Regardless of the way in which student progress is reported to the parents in the school you are teaching, it is imperative that you keep a record of all student work that is to be evaluated. If a regular teacher's grade book is not available for you, make a class-record sheet for each of the classes you teach.

GUIDELINES FOR DEVELOPING EVALUATION TECHNIQUES

Since this chapter deals with several ideas on various kinds of evaluation, the following guidelines are presented for your consideration:

1. Evaluation calls for careful planning, presentation, and follow-up. This means that you will need to make up some sort of format that will include the nature of the evaluation techniques to do the particular job you have in mind.

2. Do not expect any student to succeed beyond his own limitations. However, every student should show evidence of succeeding in something that he is doing.

3. Do not expect to discover immediately all the techniques necessary for a complete evaluation. Make use of those techniques at hand that will do the best job for you at the present time.

4. Expect some evaluations to take longer than others. Evaluating an English lesson is certainly less time-consuming than evaluating an English program for a semester or longer.

5. Avoid jumping at conclusions on the basis of a few examples.

6. Remain close to the problem of evaluation at hand. Too little data about too much are of little value in firming up sound conclusions.

7. Do not overlook a student's verbalism during his self-evaluation. This will give

you and him an opportunity to rewrite the generalization several times before agreement is reached.

8. Do not ignore an off-beat question, answer, or suggestion from a student. Take them in stride until more data are available.

9. Show surprise and elation whenever students complete their self-evaluation. There is no better way for you as the teacher to establish the proper atmosphere for future self-evaluation.

10. The most important guideline is practice. Do not be discouraged on your first attempts at evaluation. The more practice you put into evaluation, the greater the probability of success.

The following is an example of one type of class record you might want to follow in keeping your pupils' progress:

SUGGESTED CLASS RECORD

TERM

CLASS _____ TEACHER _____ DATES _____ , 19__to

GRADE _____ SUBJECT_____   _____ , 19__ .

Distribution of Final Grades						
No. in Class	A	B	C	D	E	Inc.

NAMES OF STUDENTS		1st week				2nd week				3rd week				4th week				5th week			
		M	T	W	T	F	M	T	W	T	F	M	T	W	T	F	M	T	W	T	F

REFERENCES

Veldman, D. J. "Pupil evaluation of student teachers and their supervisors," *Journal of Teacher Education,* Summer 1970, 21:165-7.

McReynolds, G. M. "When you praise the good," *School and Community,* May 1971, 54:34.

Craig, D. G. "Microteaching, to improve teacher education," *Agriculture Education,* January 1969, 41:170.

Thomas, D. "Five clues to a good school," *The American School Board Journal,* December 1970, 68:23-5.

Index

K